100 YEARS IN AMERICA

A History of a Jewish family a century after Immigration

Mark Weiss Shulkin MD

TORAH ARK
carved by Abraham Shulkin 1899

iUniverse, Inc.
Bloomington

100 Years In America
A History of a Jewish family a century after Immigration

iUniverse books may be ordered through booksellers or by contacting:

iUniverse
1663 Liberty Drive
Bloomington, IN 47403
www.iuniverse.com
1-800-Authors (1-800-288-4677)

ISBN: 978-1-4620-1041-7 (pbk)
ISBN: 978-1-4620-1042-4 (cloth)
ISBN: 978-1-4620-1043-1 (ebk)

Printed in the United States of America

iUniverse rev. date: 5/5/2011

Acknowledgement

I am grateful to my life partner and wife, Sunny Shulkin for her support during my preoccupation in writing this book as well as for her contribution to its content. Gailya Paliga was especially helpful and generous with her time in proofreading and editing.

My brother, Dick Shulkin, was helpful in his enthusiastic prodding of my memory as was his wife, Sydelle, in her comments. Our cousin Dick Zimmerman provided family data and a story of his own.

I want to thank my children Nedra Fetterman and David Shulkin, daughter in law Merle Shulkin, and my grandchildren Benjamin Fetterman, Daniel Shulkin and Jennifer Shulkin for their contribution of articles. I need to appreciate my son in law, Joseph Fetterman, for his interest in the project and for being my good friend.

Also much appreciated are those other family and friends whose contributions you see in the book, including among others, Randall Shulkin and Sandra Shulkin, (Boston branch), Diane Borkon, (Wisconsin branch), Lilian Shulkin, (New York branch), and Marlene Shulkin, Gary Sky, Jerome Shulkin, Bill Zimmerman and Ilene Zimmermann, (all of the Iowa branch).

Mark Shulkin (Mark@markshulkin.com)

Contents

Cover Story

Abraham Shulkin's Arks

In 1899, Abraham Shulkin, a Sioux City junk peddler and father of twelve, carved an ark for his Orthodox Russian Jewish synagogue, Adas Jeshurin. Carved into the wood are the inscriptions "This is the handiwork of Abraham Shulkin" and farther down below the tablets and a pair of doves, "This ark was donated by Simha, the daughter of esteemed David Davidson". Davidson owned Davidson's Department Store and he gifted Abraham with the pine lumber for the ark, which Abraham accepted in lieu of payment. Wood was not as readily available in Sioux City as it had been in well-forested Eastern Europe.

The ark is now a museum piece but in 1954 it looked like trash and in fact another Ark Abraham had built in 1909 after he had switched his synagogue membership toTifereth Israel had been dismantled and cut up for firewood.

Holy arks for synagogues at the time were without exception built by non Jewish craftsman, often German, Czech or Scandinavian but about a dozen of Adas Jeshurin's congregants had personally carved their temple's woodwork, including pew ends, book rests and tables. They carved or painted their initials on their handiwork. Perhaps it was a money saving endeavor or perhaps a matter of pride in workmanship.

Tradition of Torah

All aspects of Jewish life are based on the first five books of the Hebrew Bible and ongoing rabbinic interpretation. They are hand-written on parchment in Torah scrolls and are read in the synagogue on the Sabbath and on Mondays and Thursdays. When not in use, the Torah is kept in a Torah ark (cabinet) set against a wall facing east toward Jerusalem.

Eighteenth and nineteenth century Eastern European arks, most of them with similar icons of an eagle, tablets of the law, and hands clasped in priestly fashion were destroyed during WWII making this one particularly valuable.

Adas Jeshurin's dilapidated building and all its contents were sold to a church group in 1955 and the church, not knowing about the value of the ark, generously offered to let the former owners salvage anything they wanted from the building. As a Jewish Federation committee was about to leave the old *Shul* without salvaging anything, one of its members, Margaret Singer, (Samuel Shulkin's daughter) mentioned that her grandfather had built the ark there. (Other grandchildren were Frances Rosenberg and Ernest Shulkin.)

Grime and rubbish had covered everything so the ark didn't look like much on superficial examination. But on close inspection its artistic talent surfaced. The door panels were intricately carved with Jewish designs. There were the three dimensional precisely carved doves and intricate hands with divided fingers in priestly blessing position. An opinion sought from the director of the Sioux City Art Center was that the ark was very valuable and especially so because it was made by an unschooled amateur.

Photographs of the Shulkin ark were sent to the Chicago Art Institute, whose director wrote, "From the photographs, I am impressed with the carvings, especially the hands. Untaught work which rises above the ordinary is rare and in my book always worth preserving." He recommended contacting the Jewish Museum on upper Fifth Avenue in New York.

The Jewish Museum in New York said it would accept the ark if the Federation decided to donate it and eventually the curator sent $93.45 for its careful dismantling and shipment. It arrived in New York on October 26, 1956. The Museum restored the ark and displayed it with lamps behind it giving it a golden glow.

But in 1966, the Museum re-consecrated the ark and sent it off to its affiliate, the Sanctuary of the University of Judaism in Los Angeles. Interestingly they had not consulted the Jewish Federation in Sioux City about their decision to do that. (But then again the Federation had not consulted the Christian church which had purchased Adas Jeshurin's building along with its ark about their decision to send the ark to New York.)

Meanwhile, someone in Sioux City thought to rescue the Tifereth Israel ark that was being stored as firewood along side the boiler. It was carefully restored and eventually displayed at the Jewish Community Center in a lighted glass case. The plan was to display it at the Sioux City Jewish Community Centennial celebration in 1969. And most of it was displayed there. In early 1968, Abraham's grandchildren, Ernest and Frances, requested and were given three of its panels to be placed permanently in their St. Louis temple's museum.

Note: Abraham's having left Adas Jeshurin to join Tifereth Israel, even after having built the ark there, was not all that strange. In 1954, there were five synagogues in Sioux City, three of them Orthodox. The problem was that Orthodox Jews, having come from different parts of Eastern Europe, had different customs and degrees of orthodoxy. Their debates about rituals would be so bitterly fought that it was easier, to split off into new synagogues rather than compromise or agree (if they had the ten men required for a *minion*). The smaller congregations resulting had difficulty raising funds to maintain their buildings or to support a full-time rabbi.

In the 1950's Rabbi Saul Bolotnik served all three Orthodox synagogues, rotating between them on the Sabbath and on Jewish holidays. The other problem was that no one synagogue was large enough for an even average sized Bar Mitvah or wedding. Being 'over-templed' because of the splitting off into smaller congregations was not unique to Sioux City but was a frequent occurrence in mid-western cities with small Jewish populations.

Jim Shulkin commented:
"Thank you, Mark, for researching this remarkable story. Denise and I collect outsider art, art forms where Abraham Shulkin is a well known contributor. I'd love to see his work someday. "

Jim Shulkin and Denise Shulkin

Reply: Sorry Jim, you can't see it since it's no longer on display at an Art Museum but is in use at a Los Angeles synagogue. You'd have to attend a religious service there to see it even from a distance. The Jewish Museum betrayed the intent of the donors. The ark belongs in a museum or at least in the synagogue of one of Abe's descendants.

Jerome Shulkin commented:
"My daughter Shellie and I both strongly believe the Ark is in the Jewish Museum in NYC (earlier it was at University of Judaism). I first saw it at the University and noticed the brass plate spelling "Schulkin". Later, when I was on the board of Mercer Island JCC, a representative of the University was looking for donations. I gave him money with the condition that the nameplate be spelled right "Shulkin".It was done, and later I saw it at the NY Jewish Museum. So did Shellie."

Prologue

Gabrielle Giffords

As this book was being written in January 2011, Congresswoman Gabrielle Giffords was shot by a young paranoid schizophrenic while she was leading a political rally in a Tucson supermarket parking lot. The bullet passed through her forehead and she not only survived but as of this writing is continuing to remarkably improve in a Houston Rehabilitation Center. She has the use of all four limbs but the treatment for her loss of speech and intellectual function is just beginning. We hope and pray for her full recovery.

No. Even though Abraham Shulkin's Sioux City great grandson Robert Shulkin was married to Anne Gifford, we are not related to Congresswoman Gabrielle Giffords.

Gabrielle Giffords

We couldn't be. According to the <u>Jewish Daily Forward</u>, her grandfather, the son of a Lithuanian rabbi, was born Akiva Hornstein. He changed his name first to Gifford Hornstein and later to Gifford Giffords to shield himself and his family from anti-Semitism out West.*

Gabrielle Giffords grew up in an interfaith family, the daughter of a Jewish father and a Christian Scientist mother. Her interest in Judaism was heightened during her first trip to Israel, in 2001, shortly after the September 11 terrorist attacks and at the height of the *Second Intifada*. The trip was sponsored by the American Jewish Committee's Project Interchange, which sends politicians, journalists and opinion leaders to meet with their counterparts in the Jewish state. At the time she was a member of the Arizona state legislature.

What drew Giffords to Judaism? According to Rabbi Aaron of her synagogue was "the concept of "*tzedek, tzedek, tirdof*" — or the Jewish pursuit of justice. The way Giffords approached public service was rooted in Jewish values."

"It was a profound experience [for me] to reconnect with that philosophical approach to life and to humanity, and to look at the big picture and understand our interconnectedness," Giffords said in a 2007 interview with Jewish Woman Magazine. "I was raised not to really talk about my religious beliefs. Going to Israel was an experience that made me realize there were lots of people out there who shared my beliefs and values and spoke about them openly."

That trip to the Jewish state, a land of contradiction, of complexity and simplicity, as she called it, proved to be transformative. After she returned, she became a member of a Tucson Congregation and she met, one-on-one, every few months with Rabbi Aaron, with whom she remained close and who she frequently invited to give the invocation at local events where she was speaking.

In 2002, Giffords decided to have a formal Hebrew naming ceremony, at which she took on the name "Gabriella." Several years later, Rabbi Aaron officiated at Giffords's marriage to NASA astronaut Mark Kelly. Although the groom wasn't Jewish, Aaron said the two had a "traditional Jewish wedding, with a very beautiful *chuppah*."

Like most American Jews, Giffords seems more interested in the cultural and spiritual aspect of Judaism than in any brand of strict religious observance. I've had the thought that she might not be living today if she had adopted her mother's Christian Science upbringing. I also wonder how much her grandfather's experience with anti-Semitism influenced her political philosophy.

Note: * Rodney Dangerfield was born with the surname Cohen. He also felt better about himself using pseudonyms, once telling a TV audience that his real name was Percival Sweetwater.

Preface

Hopefully, the experiences of my family's past four to five generations in America is typical enough of yours that in reading this book you'll sense a connection with your own past history. To know one's past is to know one's self. Not knowing it, lends to risking either reliving it or rebelling against it in a self-defeating way rather than a positive way.

Recently I read that a Jewish MIT professor, guest lecturing in 1970 Warsaw, visited a nearby town that was his father's birthplace. Unfortunately his father had never told him anything about the old country and his only impression of the town was of a beautiful cathedral. How unfortunate to experience unfamiliar landmarks on visits to one's cultural past or to one's geographic past.

I was inspired to research my family by Alex Haley's <u>Roots</u> in the 1970's and prior to that by changes in psychiatric thinking during my training to be a psychiatrist in the late 1950's. I'd been born professionally into the psychoanalytic movement which avoided family contact, encouraging intrapsychic exploration to the neglect of the social aspects of neurosis.

In the family therapy movement that followed (and opposed it), some of my teachers favored bringing parents into the sessions to study their histories while other teachers favored sending the patient back home (after a year of therapy preparing for it) to have dialogues with them. I did both and doing so began collecting this data.

I hope this book encourages people to quiz their parents about the past while the opportunity is there to do so.

The book is organized chronologically to describe significant events in my family's history. The last chapter is about the recent past and I have had the good fortune of current family members being willing to write about their current interests and activities.

You can check out relationships between the people in these stories on **www. Shulkinfamily.myheritage.com** Go to **Family Tree** and click on **People.** The names are listed alphabetically. Then click on **Family Tree.**

CHAPTER ONE

Generations Ago

THE VALUE OF FAMILY HISTORY

Life in the old country was hard for Jews but a hard life stimulates positive character traits, traits passed down to descendants.

For example: My dog Buddy, a Shetland Sheep Dog, is obsessed with herding though he's never seen a sheep.

According to Dr. Ivan Boszenmenyi-Nagz and Geraldine Spark authors of <u>INVISIBLE LOYALTIES</u>, people also are programmed to act out the experiences of their ancestors, They write that we are psychological accountants keeping a mental ledger of the good and the bad that preceded us and that we need to pay the good forward and seek revenge for, or undo, the bad.

I think that's true. I was named after my Dad's maternal grandfather, Maer Baer Gelman (Choolimienov), a "*feldscher*" who practiced folk medicine illegally since he had no medical training or license. Jews were not allowed to attend institutions of higher learning after Czar Alexander's 1881 assassination was falsely attributed to Jewish revolutionaries.

Grandpa Maer lived in fear of the Russian police who repeatedly invaded his home looking for illegal drugs as proof of his practicing medicine without a license. Fortunately the town folk appreciated his medical care and warned him whenever he was about to be raided.

So eight of his descendants that I personally know of, have become licensed physicians (John and Eugene Usow, Dave and Abe Sverdlin, Milt Spitz, David Shulkin, Frank Shulkin and me) but not a single one has become a police officer.

Other examples of "invisible loyalties" are Sunny Shulkin's cousins, Peter Edelman and Marian Wright Edelman. Peter is the grandson of Rabbi Eliezer Edelman, who was the Chief Rabbi in Rubiezewisc, Poland when the Nazis invaded and planned to exterminate the entire Jewish community. The Rabbi and his wife volunteered to be executed in their place and they were publically shot to death in the town square.

Peter, a close friend of Hilary Clintons since they were in law school together, had accepted an appointment in Health and Human Services during the Clinton administration but he resigned abruptly, protesting Clinton's signing a budget bill that reduced the welfare rolls from 15 million to 4 million and charged penniless people $2.00 for their food stamps. That was a selfless occupational sacrifice.

His wife Marian Wright Edelman is also selflessly motivated. As an unknown lawyer for a Mississippi Child Development group, she was called before Senator Robert Kennedy's Senate committee in Washington to testify about a need for the Head Start Program. Under oath, she refused to testify saying that she could not talk about Head Start when children were starving in Mississippi.

Senator Kennedy was not pleased with her. No one believed it possible that children could be starving in America, but Mrs. Edelman led Senator Kennedy and a CBS reporter to Mississippi to see such children themselves. That evening, national television showed pictures of children with bloated bellies and sores on their skin. The publicity quickly led to Kennedy sponsored welfare legislation that alleviated the situation.

Marian Wright Edelman is founder and president of the Children's Defense League, and can trace her ancestry back to slavery.

Note: In the mid 1980's, Sunny and I met the Edelmans at a spa in Baja California when Sunny recognized Marian from having seen pictures of her. During the conversation, I probably offended her when in response to her question about whether we lived in Philadelphia proper. Fancying myself a humorist, I replied that we lived in the suburbs and that "No one lives in Philadelphia proper".

Marian Wright Edelman

THE FELDSCHER

My choice of psychiatry as a specialty in medicine was pre-determined by my being named after my paternal great grandfather, Maer Baer Gelman, the "*feldscher*" who practiced folk medicine; folk medicine being a more psychological than physiological practice.

I remember my Dad, Joe Shulkin, telling me about his childhood, accompanying Maer Baer as he bartered his medical services for chickens, eggs and bushels of corn or wheat. I still picture myself sitting, shotgun style, along side Maer Baer as he drove his horse and wagon through the countryside. The wagon I picture is the wagon my junk peddler maternal grandfather, Jacob Weiss, treated me to rides on in Milwaukee.

Folk Remedies

Grandpa Maer Baer was a popular healer even if he did not have a medical degree. His patients would have preferred his folk medicine practice even if licensed doctors were available to them. That generation had little faith in traditional medicine.*

Feldschers treated Small Pox (Chicken Pox?) by burying the person up to his neck in the ground. Though this is hard to believe, I imagine it reduced fever and prevented scratching.

Aspirin, the wonder drug of that time**, was not yet available to Grandpa, having been first marketed by the German Bayer Company in 1899 only through pharmacies in powder form to be compressed by them into tablets. It was an ethical drug rather than a patent medicine and available only by prescription of physicians.

Grandpa Maer used leeches for infection. For indigestion, he prescribed "cupping", lighting a match under a glass creating a vacuum that brought blood to the surface of the skin, else a mustard plaster" which on removal had the same effect. Sometimes these treatments were effective, if only for their hypnotic suggestion, but other times not. The theory was that in removing even minimal blood this way, the bad substances of the body were removed, leaving the good stuff.

He liked steaming hot teas for colds, which probably loosened the phlegm, relieved nasal congestion and increased the immune response. For tooth ache, he prescribed a bitter mix of garlic and salt water followed by a glass of wine to kill the taste. Probably it was the wine that was most effective but there is current research that "allicin," a component of garlic, disables the enzymes needed by bacteria to invade cells.

Raw egg white was applied to soothe sunburn or oozing circumcisions.

Grandpa liked to prescribe herbs and natural foods.*** Fennel was to prevent miscarriage. Cranberries, which may have helped by changing the acidity of the urine, relieved urinary tract infection. Pomegranates, now known for their antioxidant power, along with seaweed, cabbage, broccoli, radishes and high doses of tomatoes were prescribed to prevent breast cancer.

Notes:
* If a child was seriously ill, it was the custom to take the child to a synagogue where, with a minion of 10 men, a ritual renaming the child would be chanted. The new name would be used on all legal documents. The old one, if listed at all, would be listed as an alias. New names were often Chaim (life), Alte (the elder), or Zede (grandfather). Then when the Angel of Death came to the house looking for the child he'd be fooled into thinking that no such child lived there.

My Grandma Sosha Shulkin died of untreated diabetic coma in the early 1930's. When my Grandpa Malech Shulkin, at 90, was admitted to Milwaukee County Hospital in 1957 with fatal cancer of the esophagus, he resisted being treated in the hospital because of the feeling of his generation that hospitals were places where you went to die. He agreed to go only under the condition that my Uncle Henry list his age on admission as 60, thinking that would better motivate the doctors to try to save him. I read his hospital chart when I visited him. The admitting physician's note described him as "a 60 year old man who looks 30 years older than his stated age, admitted to the hospital by his family probably as a matter of disposition".

** In 1912, young Alexander III, Czar apparent and a hemophiliac, was injured in an assassination attempt. His doctors tried to stop his bleeding with Aspirin which, not yet known to be an anticoagulant, made things worse. He was eventually helped by the faith healer, Rasputin, whose prayers and incantations may have relaxed him and lowered his blood pressure hypnotically.

Rasputin, a anti-Semitic renegade monk, advised the Royal family to solve the "Jewish Problem" by converting a third using military conscription, executing a third, and encouraging the other third to emigrate.

ELLIS ISLAND

Life in America began on arrival at one of the East Coast seaports. One out of six native Americans can trace an ancestor's immigration to Castle Garden between 1855 and 1890 and another three out of the six to Ellis Island from 1892 to 1924.* Others, like my grandfather Jacob Weiss, disembarked in ports like Philadelphia, where he and other steerage passengers waited their turn to be processed aboard ship while first class passengers were ferried ashore. (Weiss was the Yiddish translation of Bellacherkevsky which was too hard for the immigration officials to spell. Bella is white and cherkev is church in Russian)

Quebec City was the entry point for Jake Shulkin who bought a combined steamship and railway ticket from the Canadian Pacific Railway and on arrival in Canada took the train to his destination in New York. My father in law, Sam Edelman, landed in Galveston Texas as part of a plan to settle Jewish immigrants west of the Mississippi.

Castle Gardens was an army fort on the tip of southern Manhattan, built during the War of 1812 to protect New Yorkers from a British invasion. Currently the building still stands, maintained by the National Park Service and is the ticket office for ferries to the Statue of Liberty and to Ellis Island, New York's most popular tourist attraction.

I toured Ellis Island in 1970 before its restoration and found its main hall to be dreary and dilapidated. I could sense the terror felt by immigrants still on its upper level waiting to pass physical exams at threat of children and parents being separated if an illness required one of them to be sent back to their native country.

Imagine them being herded into the polyglot of languages spoken on the lower level. First thing to do was to change your European money for dollars without any idea of the exchange rate. Then they had to buy food, since it was no longer being supplied by the steamship company. They purchased it in a cafeteria line that served 3000 lunches daily. Not speaking English, they had no choice as to what the server would put in a brown paper bag for them or at what cost. Nor did they know whether it would last until their next destination.

Still this must have seemed less torturous than the three weeks in steerage with poor sanitation and little ventilation while at the mercy of ocean waves and foul weather. My grandmother, Dora Weiss, was said to have given birth to my Uncle Izzy at sea. She was nauseous and she vomited during the entire voyage.

Both Castle Gardens and Ellis Island kept good records which are available now free of charge on the internet. If your surname is not too common of a one, all you need is its phonetic spelling and you are rewarded with a list of people by that name who passed through, along with the city they came from, the vessel they traveled on, their age, and their date of their arrival. If you already know one or more of these items and enter it, the list returned is limited to likely relatives. It's a convenient way to start a genealogy search.

Having the name of the ship and date of arrival* is the entre' to a similar computer readout from the National Archives that lists ships' passengers, how much money they brought along and who their sponsors were at their final destination in America. Knowing their destination city and age, gives you census bureau readouts and then city vital statistics and city phone books access,

Immigration officials as well as the assimilation process play loosely with given names. I found my Uncle Henry listed as Henle, and my Uncle Max as Michal. Uncle Max was re-named by his fourth grade teacher in predominantly German Milwaukee's rigid school system because she felt that Michael was an Irish name and she insisted on changing it to the more appropriately Jewish sounding Max on his school records. That seems small compared to immigration officials in South Africa mistaking the sch or sj sounding Greek Cyrillic alphabet character, Yatch, for the Greek letter Omega and permanently misnaming the South African Shulkins "Wolkin."

Note: * The Milwaukee Shulkin family arrived December 1, 1910 on the S.S. Lithuania, which sank two years later in a Titanic like incident.

THE FOURTH STREET SCHOOL

The Fourth Street School still stands at 4th and Galena Streets in Milwaukee though several wings have been added and it's been renamed the Golda Meier School. It's now a magnet school for gifted children.

My mother, as Marion Weiss, was a student there from 1908 to 1916. One of her schoolmates was Golda Mapovich, 1897-1971, who shortened and Hebrewcized her married name from Myerson to Meier before becoming Prime Minister of Israel.

The Weisses and the Mabovitches were *Landtsman* who felt a kinsmanship to each other because they came from the same area of Russia, a *shtetl* near Kiev. Better off than the Weisses, the Mabovitches lived above their 5th Street grocery store. Golda was often the one watching the store when Marion went there as a customer.

Golda and Marion had the "benefit" of the Germanic discipline typical of Milwaukee, where German language was required in all the primary schools grades. At the Fourth Street School, discipline was strict. As an example, in the cloak room boots were required to be neatly placed under one's coat with toes all neatly pointed toward the center of the room.

Mark Weiss Shulkin MD

MARGARET SANGER

At the turn of the century, genetics was a scientific breakthrough stimulating a continuing research that eventually turned out to have fatal consequences. Bad research along with birth control proponents like Margaret Sanger was a factor in millions of tragic deaths during the Holocaust.

It all started in 1882 with Mendel's laws concerning the relationship of genes to the heredity of peas. By1900, the principles of genetics had been extended to other plants and eventually to humans. But all this was before the discovery of DNA markers and the research was limited to observations about a succeeding generation's similarities to its parents and grandparents.

The method wasn't all that bad in studying inanimate species or even in those humans who had large families. In fact it was later to be effective in tracing familial traits of Bipolar Disorder in the Amish. But with the tendency to use smaller families and institutions, the research switched to the study of prisons, insane asylums, homes for the blind, orphanages and even circuses where polydactism, hypertrichosis, gigantism and dwarfism were studied.

That was not good Scientific Method. In changing the venue from large families, the focus of the research shifted to the ethnic origin of the persons and to vague definitions of the concepts studied. When used to test the IQ's of recruits inducted into the service in WW I, researchers falsely concluded lower intelligence in foreign born recruits as opposed to native American recruits without considering that good IQ test scores depended on fluency in English. The publications were short on data and long on anecdotal material, allowing researchers to skew the material in favor of their political views.

Margaret Sanger was an early advocate of women's rights whose efforts added to the tragic outcome brought on by eugenics. The Susan B. Anthony, the Gloria Steinem and the Betty Friedan of her time, she was a political activist for birth control over a 50 year span. She firmly believed that over procreation was the cause of her own family's poverty and the poverty of inner city women,

Mrs. Sanger's writings espoused her interest in eugenics and sterilization along with birth control as a means for improving the race. She recommended sterilization for mental defectives, sexual deviates and the chronically insane without consideration of who was to make such judgments.

At best, this thinking was insensitive to the feelings of oppressed minorities. Black people who were being lynched in the South, for instance, were particularly threatened by the implications that the human race could be bettered by eugenics. At worst, eugenics encouraged the Nazis in their belief in the superiority of Nordic people with blond hair and blue eyes.

This belief in the superiority of light skinned people from northern Europe was reflected in the Immigration Acts of 1913, 1917 and 1924 which governed United States immigration policy until 1952. They established a quota system which mandated that immigration from any country be limited to 2% of that country's foreign born population existing in the United States at the time of the 1890 census.

From 1881- 1890 only 15% of immigrants were of South Eastern European origin. The wave of Russian Jewish immigration from 1901-1910 changed that to 75%. After the immigration acts, the percentage in 1931-1940 had fallen to only 35% from South-eastern European countries. Specifically it favored light skinned German, Irish and English people, for whom there was no quota, over the darker skins of many Jewish and Italian immigrants. The act completely halted immigration of "undesirables" from Japan, China, the Philippines, Laos, Thailand, Korea, Vietnam, Burma, India, Sri Lanka, and Malaysia. Forget Africa.

The influx of Jews to the eastern coastal cities so aroused concern about immigration changing the complexion of America that in 1907, that my father in law, Sam Edelman's financial aid from the HIAS, Hebrew Immigration Aid Society, depended on his signing an agreement that he would settle west of the Mississippi River.

The contempt for immigrants was reflected in derogatory names hurled at them. Jews were called *"Kikes"*- stemming from their signing their names at Ellis Island with a circle (*kikel* in Yiddish), rather than an X which they associated with the Christian cross. Italians were called Dagos because they mostly had day jobs in which their pay would depend on how much of the day the job lasted. So they were paid according to how the "day goes". The term Wop was an acronym for "with out papers".

Italian immigrants were not much offended by these terms but if you wanted to get your ass kicked, all you had to do was call an Italian American a

"Guinea." That referred to their darker skin being associated to that of the natives of the African country of Guinea.

Prior to our entry into WWII, many gentile Americans believed that Jewish groups were encouraging them to get into the war even though it had been "caused" by the greedy practices of the international Jewish bankers, like the Rothschilds and Morgenthaus. Along with a tendency to believe theories of racial inferiority, this reinforced America's isolationist policy. The effect was to prevent Jewish refugees from finding asylum in the United States and to cause the deaths of millions of innocent people.

Note: Interest in genetics was so popular at the time that many Americans sought "expert" advice on the choice of marriage partners. My nearsighted father was advised by his genetics professor at the University of Wisconsin to be sure to marry a woman with normal vision for the sake of his children. (He eventually married my mother because she was "good looking".)

IS ISRAEL'S CLAIM TO PALESTINE VALID?

(Genomology vs Genealogy)

Is Israel's claim to Palestine justified by its belief that their land was a gift from God to His Chosen People, the descendents of Abraham?

The Israeli historian and professor of history at Tel Aviv University, Shlomo Sand, in his book "The Invention of the Jewish People" cites Y-chromosome genetic studies that indicate that Jews have no common origin but were a miscellany of people in Europe and Central Asia who converted to Judaism at various times.

Two new genetic surveys extend earlier studies based just on the Y chromosome, the genetic element carried only in men, refute the suggestion made by Sand. This data indicates that members of any Jewish community are genetically related to one another as closely as are fourth or fifth cousins in a large population. That is about 10 times higher than the relationship between two people chosen at random off the streets of New York City.

The surveys, the first to use genome-wide scanning devices to compare many Jewish communities around the world, show the genetic closeness of the two Jewish communities of Europe, the Ashkenazim (Ancient Hebrew for Germans) and the Sephardim (ancient Hebrew for Spaniards). The Ashkenazim thrived in Northern and Eastern Europe until their devastation by the Hitler regime, and they now live mostly in the United States and Israel. The Sephardim were exiled from Spain in 1492 and from Portugal in 1497 and moved to the Ottoman Empire, North Africa and the Netherlands. The Ashkenazi community spoke Yiddish, and the Sephardim community spoke Ladino. When these Jews met each other, they spoke Hebrew.

The two communities seem very similar to each other genetically, which is unexpected because they have been separated for so long. The genomic signature of Ashkenazim and Sephardim is also very similar to that of Italian Jews, suggesting that an ancient (800A.D.) Jewish population in northern Italy that intermarried with Italians could have been the common origin.

COURAGE OF THE PIONEERS

by Dick Zimmermann

Dick Zimmermann

My Zimmermann grandparents survived very well without learning one word of English despite living in the United States for over 30 years. They had come here from Vitebsk, Belarus, in 1912, and continued to speak Yiddish and Russian until they died. They lived a few houses down the street from us in San Antonio, Texas in the mid to late 1940s.

Dad was only four at the time they made the crossing, and he claimed his only memory of the voyage was when he came up on deck to see the Statue of Liberty and his hat blew over the side of the ship. [Many years after he passed away, I found out that they had entered through Philadelphia on the ship *Dominion* and didn't come through Ellis Island, so the Statue of Liberty reference was bogus. An understandable error from someone who was four years old at the time.] The family remained in Philadelphia, and my father quit school after the sixth grade to go to work to help support the family. My grandfather worked as a tailor in Philadelphia, like so many other immigrant Jews who worked in the garment industry.

Dad's parents were Grandpop Mitch and Grandma Rosie to us, and we used to visit them at least once a week – even when we moved away in the late 1940s and they were no longer just down the street. I remember best the great strawberries they grew in their back yard. I also remember that visits always included one or two 'schnapps' for Grandpop and for Dad. Mother would often tell Dad "You never take me anywhere" to which he would answer, "We'll go visit my parents." I doubt that she had that in mind when she registered her complaint.

Dick, Rose, Jack, and Michol Zimmermann 1944

Even now in 2011, I still remember very well the washing 'machine' they had, which consisted of a tub, a washboard, and a hand-driven wringer. There was no electricity involved. That was the only wringer I ever saw in a home, and I even saw Grandma Rosie use it a few times. They kept it in their kitchen near a window, and I can still picture it now. Grandma would fill the washtub with a hose from the kitchen sink, wash the clothes with the washboard, and run them through the wringer to get most of the water out. Then she would hang the clothes on a line in the backyard. We have home movies of both Grandpop and Grandma bringing in the clothes from the clothesline in a hurry as a rainstorm was starting up.

I don't think Grandpop would help much with the laundry in the absence of a storm. He was very dignified as I recall, and I never saw him wearing anything but a three-piece suit. He was even wearing a suit when helping bring in the clothes, so I was somewhat surprised when I saw the photo of him with no tie or jacket in *Search for the Family*, published in 1980 by Sack and Shulkin.

We used to eat at our grandparents' home every now and then, and Grandma was famous for her *borscht* soup. I was never a big fan of *borscht*, but I ate it anyway as she seemed to be very proud of it and everyone else seemed to like it. I vaguely remember getting Hanukkah *gelt* in the form of those chocolate coins from Grandpop Mitch, but that was the extent of our presents from grandparents. None of them could afford the luxury of presents, and there were lots of us grandkids.

Cousin Rose Seigel told me this story of the Old Country that her mother Edith, who was born in Philadelphia, told her. I laughed uncontrollably when I heard it. The story went like this: 'They kept Kosher and the *Shechet* only came to the village periodically. When he came, they would slaughter the animals, put the meat into a big barrel, and fill it with water. The water would then freeze. When Grandma wanted something for dinner, Grandpa would go to the barrel and chop the ice with an ax. Whatever he broke off, they would have for dinner.' I guess that was similar in many ways to the deep-freeze units that came along many years later after the family had resettled in the United States.

The name Zimmerman was Tsinman in the Old Country. My Aunt Sonia (a diminutive for her actual name Sophie) was born in the *shtetl* Paperniya in 1894. My Aunt Masha was born in Disna in 1896, and my father was born in Paperniya in 1908. Seven others were born in various *shtetls* in the Vitebsk area. The Tsinmans were bouncing from *shtetl* to *shtetl* so frequently that I'm not sure how anyone ever figured out where each of the ten children was born, but it's all there in *Search for the Family.*

The great artist Marc Chagall was born in 1887 as Moishe Shagal, in Liozna, another *shtetl* near Vitebsk. I often wonder if my grandparents had crossed paths with his family anywhere along the line.

Can today's family members be appropriately grateful and properly impressed with the courage of those pioneers of the early twentieth century? Setting out for the United States must have been more frightening than we'll ever appreciate, despite how bad it must have been under the Czar. Crossing the ocean was difficult for someone from a small *shtetl* to do, despite the hardships they experienced in the Pale of Settlement, which is why it required people with the pioneer spirit to take those first steps. Regardless of how bad a known place might be, the unknown for many of us is even more frightening. But they took that plunge and in doing so, they saved us all from the nightmares we would have experienced had they not boldly come across the ocean. Most of our forefathers came from places that were virtually wiped out in World War II.

Note: I wrote a semi-fictional story to try to convey what these brave immigrants went through, both in Russia and here in the United States. The story includes my grandparents in Vitebsk in the background with only a minor role, and can be found on the internet at the following link: http://www.online-literature.com/forums/showthread.php?t=30993.

THE ARGENTINE FAMILY

Argentina as well as the United States and Israel was the destination for some of our relatives. I'd been puzzling about the South American Shulkins for some time without success partly because I'm terrible at Spanish and partly because the "New Generation" of Argentineans, like their North American counterparts, have assimilated and they seem to lack my fascination with family history. But happily, their interest in Ron and Jacob Shulkin's "Shulkin Facebook page" (at http://www.facebook.com/group.php?gid=2229326672 &ref=search&sid=1313276927.3191736203..1) with its over 100 registrants from the United States, Canada, France, Germany, Russia, Israel, Uruguay, Argentina, Iran, and Indonesia helped solve the mystery.

When Sergio Shulkin from Buenos Aires wrote that Dov Baer Rosen was a familiar family name, it suggested a relationship to my great grandmother, Gelye Dvorah Shulkin whose father was Yankel Baer Rosen. Her brother, Raphael Rosen, had emigrated to Argentina.

Then Ile Levinson's note on Christmas Day 2009 and her sister Tamara Levinson's message the next month, was a Uruguayan connection. They wrote that their mother's maiden name was Schulkin and that they were related to the Rosens.

Add to this that five Rosens were listed on the ship's manifest of the SS. Weser (or Barco Veser Vapor), debarking in Buenos Aires in 1889. Though Raphael Rosen was not one of them, he may have been the David Rosen, having taken the name of his young nephew, pseudonyms being a Jewish emigration custom of the times in order to avoid military conscription and the paying of back taxes. (David on later immigrating could have taken the name Raphael.)

My great grandma Gelye Dvorah Schulkin had a son, Peretz, who went to Argentina. He had a son, Marcos Shulkin, who had sons Arturo, Abraham, Miguel, Isadore and daughters Leah and Maria. Some of them went to Uruguay sometime after the terrible week of violence toward Argentinean Jews in 1919.

Probably one of Gelye Dvorah's children was the grandparent of Ile and Tamara Levinson and of Pablo Schulkin in Montevideo. Veronica Schulkin's and Marcos' Schulkin's grandfather must have remained in Argentina.

Another of Gelye Devorah's children probably emigrated to Israel at that time or during the Zionist initiatives of the 1930's.

Some Argentine History

In 1881, President Julio A. Roca sent an emissary to Russia to promote Jewish emigration from the anti-Semitic Czar's Empire. On August 14, 1889, the first organized group of Russian Jews arrived at Buenos Aires aboard the S.S. Weser.

Although Argentina was not a very well-known country in Russia, a con man by the name of Rafael Hernández was selling lands to European immigrants. Those lands were supposedly in Buenos Aires province close to La Plata city and not far from Buenos Aires. The sales resulted in 120 Russian Jewish families moving to Argentina.

On the day they arrived in Buenos Aires, a series of misfortunes overtook them. The lands were not available and the immigrants were desperate. They lacked resources and were ignorant of the language in a strange country. They were housed in boxcars parked on the side of the railroad tracks. They waited daily to be transferred to their fields, but to no avail. Hungry children begged for food next to their parents when trains passed. An epidemic swept the area and lacking hygiene and medical attention about sixty children died.

The broken-hearted families dispersed mostly to Buenos Aires, where no work was available. Some of them returned to Russia. Only the strongest, who swore solemnly before lit candles to stay, remained.

Note: There were only a million Jews on the world in the 1700's so the small percentage of them named Shulkin or Rosen who lived or immigrated to what is now Belarus, Lithuania or the Ukraine, were most likely related. Even if that's not so, I like to think of all Jews as *mishpoche*, spiritually related, having suffered similar past experiences in their families.

CAN SHULKINS BE KOHANIM?

In the late 70's, while chasing CEU's in Texas, I found a "Shulkin" in the local phone book and scored a dinner invitation from Roger and Marlene Shulkin. They'd originated in Sioux City and had the good looks, intelligence and charm that runs in our family but they were *Kohanim* while I'm an Israelite, ruling them out as family. I considered that people lie about their tribe to get status in the temple but lying is a sin and we Shulkins are genetically incapable of sin.

Years later I heard a story about a Yahashua (Joshua) Kohen who was supported by his wealthy Shulkin father-in-law so he could study Talmud all day. *Nachus* being what it was in those days- he was referred to as Shulkin's Yahashua and when surnames were mandated he took the name of Yahashua Shulkin. That made his children *Kohanim*, though they were named Shulkin.

Sallyann Sack wrote March 25, 1982: "Mark, Do you remember the Sioux City Iowa Shulkins and how it first it seemed that they should be related since so many had the same first names that our family had –e.g Abraham. Well Randy Deutsch a Toledot correspondent reminded me last month that we still might be related even though they are Kohanim and we aren't. I mentioned it to my Rabbi friend in Jerusalem and got a reply from him yesterday. He says that it often occurred that a young *yeshiva bucher* is married to a well to do man's daughter whose name might be Shulkin.

I am trying to find out who all these Abrahams are named after. What do you say?

CHAPTER TWO
Early Twentieth Century

THE BOSTON BUNCH

Even before his Bar Mitzvah in an 1882 Polotsk, Lithuania synagogue, 13 year old Abraham Shulkin was already a man. He managed to take off for America that year all by himself, leaving family, he thought, forever.

In doing so, he escaped Czar Nicholas II's government sponsored pogroms, Russia's growing sense of pride as a military power conscripting boys into 25 years of service, and the embarrassment Abraham and his family may have felt about his impregnating a girl while too young to marry her.

Doing well in rapidly industrializing Boston, he was already Americanized and solvent by the time the large influx of Russian Jews began in the beginning of the century. He'd been able to send for his father, Zalman, for his mother and his siblings, and by 1902 he had established a family of his own.

Itsky, Abraham, Morris, Hannah and Percy Shulkin 1905

Abraham's courage and hard work are traditionally honored by the Boston Shulkins in their naming first born sons with names starting with A. Similarly they name first born daughters beginning with the initial I after Abraham's daughter, Ida, 1898-1914, who died as a teenager.*

Abraham's son, Itsky (Isadore) Shulkin, quit school at 15 to work selling newspapers on a street corner in post war 1919. Business was good and he got the idea of going into office buildings and selling them door to door with his older brothers manning the street stand. That business was even more successful and all the brothers went door to door leaving their sisters to attend the newsstand.

Allen Stationery

Then one day an office customer gave Itsky some money and asked if he'd bring some pencils the next day in return for a tip. Soon Itsky was buying pencils by the gross and the other brothers were also peddling office supplies door to door

They stored their stock in a cleaned out a coal bin at their Allen Street tenement. Next, they connected with the Carter Company and marketed already inked stamp pads and stamps. They spread out into many stationery outlets stores in the Boston area as the Allen Street Stationery Stores. In later years they merged into Litton Industries.

Family Problems

There are common problems in family businesses. My psychiatric practice over the years saw many. Typically the founder is a youngest son and he brings in his oldest son to continue after his retirement. The oldest son dominates his younger siblings who are also in the business.

Oldest sons are programmed during childhood to be the responsible child and to be the caretakers for the younger more playful, and imaginative ones. So in the business the oldest son plays a similar role and is not likely to reward the creativity or leadership efforts of the younger ones. If the oldest child in the business is a female caretaker, she is bypassed as a company officer in favor of doing secretarial work ands she works her tail off for less pay. After all, she has a husband to take care of her.

First the quarreling is limited to the office, but then factions in the families ally themselves and people learn not to speak about business in social situations. Then they stop speaking altogether and misunderstandings and accusations that have nothing to do with business prevail. Then lawyers get involved and things really escalate.

The Shulkin variation was that Itsky, the founder of the business was four and five years younger than his brothers Michol and Moe (Morris) respectively. Each of them brought in sons and grandsons as the business grew. At one point fifteen stationery company executives included siblings and their children as follows:

- Michol, his sons Arnold and Irvin Shulkin, and his grandsons Edward Shulkin and Richard Cramer
- Moe, his son Arnold Shulkin and grandsons Robert Nathans and Fred Shulkin
- Itsky, his son Alvin Shulkin and grandson Lawrence Shulkin
- Benjamin Shulkin (their youngest brother)
- Ida and Molly, the sisters who had minded the original news stands.

It was a setup for family conflict.

Fred Shulkin circa 2007 Fred Shulkin 1927

Shulkin vs Shulkin was the very first Massachusetts case of family suing family over the dissolution of a business. Coincidentally, in the Wisconsin branch of the family, Usow vs. Usow was the first Wisconsin case of family suing family over a family business.

<u>Note:</u> * I assume first daughters are named after Ida because her uncle Michol Shulkin did not follow that rule in naming his first daughter Mildred in 1910 but he named his second daughter Ida in 1914, the year of Ida's death.

ABANDONMENT BY EMIGRANT HUSBANDS

Russian Jews who fled pogroms and military conscription were poor and the cost of a steamship ticket to America was high. For a single person alone it was about 70 rubles (children under five paid five rubles and children under 12 paid half price). while the average income of a shopkeeper or tradesman varied between five and 600 rubles per year. Add to that the cost of obtaining documents, bribing officials, the train journey, accommodation at the port of departure and food expenses during the journey.

So the men often came to America first, promising to send tickets for their wives and children when they'd made enough money to do so.

It isn't possible to find statistics on how many men reneged on that promise since most of those who did couldn't be located or were reluctant to be interviewed. Those who were interviewed had lame excuses like they moved to a distant city and lost touch with the family.

There are two such instances in my family and recently a friend told me about a tavern keeper who was generously supporting his wife and children back in Italy while having established a new family in Montreal. Charitable agencies of those times have records of a multitude of women with children who were unable to locate their husbands and consequently had no means of support.

Hannah and Abe

My Grand Aunt Hannah Ritter had married Abe, a journalist in Russia before the turn of the 19th Century. They lived in Kaniev, a *shtetl* 15 miles east of Kiev along the Dniper River. After five years of marriage and the birth of their children, Esther and Morris, Abe emigrated to America promising to send for the family as soon as he found work and earned the money for the tickets. He found a job as a reporter for a Jewish newspaper in New York, fell in love with his doting secretary, and married her. A son was born a year later. Unbeknownst to his new wife, Abe wrote Hannah lame excuses, requesting that she be patient and sending small sums of money back to Russia.

One day a cousin met Abe and his new family in New York and wrote to Hannah about it. Hannah borrowed money from relatives and traveled to New York with their children to confront Abe. It was a difficult and somewhat perilous trip. Women in Russia being unable to request documents without their husband's permission, she had to leave illegally, bribing officials and hiring an agent to smuggle her across the border surreptitiously at night.

An Agunah

Under misogynous Jewish Law, or *halakah*, Hannah was now an *agunah*, (anchored in marriage) who, if she remarried, became an adulteress and any children of that union would be *momzers* (illegitimate) as would their children for the next seven generations. *Momzers* are not permitted to participate in Jewish religious services and can only marry other *momzers* or a non Jew. Under Jewish law, however, men are allowed to have children by women who are not their wives. *Halakah* also states that a wife cannot divorce a man without his consent, allowing him to hold out for unreasonable property or child custody agreements.

Hannah was a short, plump but attractive red head with green eyes and a feisty vivacious personality. She was super competent like most of the Russian Jewish women who were used to both raising children and working to support their families while their husbands either studied Torah or held low income jobs. It was not surprising that she pursued Abe.

Abe was not willing to leave his new wife and his one year old child by that marriage, so she had him arrested as a bigamist and he was imprisoned. After a few weeks, the second wife offered Hannah substantial money if she would withdraw the charges. Hannah took the money and bought a small grocery store in Chester, Pa (a thriving port on the Delaware River at the time). There she met and married Max Ritter, a single real estate broker some years her senior, who adopted Esther and Morris. After a year, they had a child of their own.

Jake

The second example is my Grand Uncle Jake Shulkin, who I knew personally though didn't know this story back then. In 1902, at age 21, Jake was drafted into the Russian Army to serve in the Russo Japanese War, even after having shot himself in the leg and suffering a limp in hopes of avoiding it. Military service was for 25 years in those days and usually meant death for Jewish boys.

Jake's two older sisters, Rose and Gussie, disguised as prostitutes, gained entrance to the army barracks and smuggled Jake out dressed as a woman.

Under the circumstances it was imperative that he leave the country shortly after that.

The problem was that his parents, through a matchmaker (*schachten*), had already arranged his marriage. The bride to be had been saving her money to set up housekeeping and to help her father with the dowry, but willingly gave Jake the money for his passage with the promise that he'd send for her as soon as he was able.

In New York, he met and fell in love with his first cousin, Sarah Saidell. He wrote to the woman in Russia asking for a release from the marriage agreement, but she was bitter and she placed a curse on him and his progeny and eventually she suicided. Jake and Sarah were to recall the curse later when their first child, Willie, came down with a mental disorder and later was arrested after seemingly confessing to the murder of a temporarily lost Christian child.

SEX IN THE CITY

After the birth of her third daughter in 1916, my Grand Aunt Yetta Benn went to see Dr. Cooper to ask him if he had any pills that would prevent her from getting pregnant again. He said that there was nothing on the market yet that was considered foolproof and safe. He told her that on certain days of the month a woman could "live with her husband and not get pregnant". Yetta felt the explanation incomprehensible and she left the office discouraged.

The problem was not language barrier. Dr. Cooper spoke fluent Yiddish. You'd have to have read TIME MAGAZINE back then to understand the doctor's vagueness.

"Congressmen last week foiled Mrs. Margaret Sanger's sixth attempt to get a Federal law passed which will allow doctors to give their patients advice on birth control without running the risk of being jailed and fined."

A few days after the office visit, Yetta read in her Yiddish newspaper that Margaret Sanger was speaking in Philadelphia about planned parenthood and that each woman attending would be given a pamphlet at the end of the meeting explaining techniques of birth control.

She went to the meeting with her cousin who had three small sons and didn't want any more children. They left home early to get good seats. The hall was crowded and in spite of being early, their seats up front were off to the side near an exit.

As Margaret Sanger was explaining that unless population was controlled the world would soon be in dire trouble, Yetta heard police sirens and a whistle blow. She looked behind her and saw that the police were coming down the aisles. They surrounded Mrs. Sanger on the stage. The cousins left hurriedly through the side exit.

In the 1910's and 1920's, the entire social order—religion, law, politics, medicine, and the media—was arrayed against the idea of and the practice of birth control. This opposition began in 1873 with the Comstock Act which listed obscene writing, along with drugs, and the advocating of devices and articles that prevented conception or caused abortion, under the same degree of criminality. Mrs. Sanger had been arrested and prosecuted many times and she served prison time under this law.

GIMBELS IN MILWAUKEE

Growing up in Milwaukee during the 30's and 40's there were three department stores, Boston Store and Gimbels both downtown, and Schusters, a low rise chain in the neighborhoods. My widowed aunt, Sophie Ahvner, worked at Gimbels and she gave our family her employee's discount for all our purchases.

Gimbels was a high rise, block long store on the Milwaukee River at Wisconsin Ave where Border's Books is now. It was founded in 1887 by German Jewish Adam Gimbel who was born in 1815 and who immigrated in 1835.

The Jewish pre-Civil War German immigrants were mostly adventurous single young men who were not fleeing persecution but were seeking economic opportunities in underdeveloped America. German Jews of the 19th century were well integrated into German society and accepted as German citizens rather than as Jews. They spoke German and not Yiddish, so they tended to settle in German speaking cities when in America.

Sioux City and Milwaukee were German speaking and booming, but there were few Jews. So it was not possible there to observe the dietary laws or the Sabbath. Jewish men often attended Unitarian Churches or Christian ones, going to larger cities for the High Holidays. Anti-Semitism had not yet been imported and they were accepted as equal citizens or even leaders of the Gentile community.

They went back to the east coast to find Jewish brides, who more than they, fostered Jewish identity in joining Hadassah or organizing local Jewish charities and extremely liberal Reformed Jewish synagogues.

Although they were generous in helping less fortunate Jewish immigrants, when the mass immigration began at the turn of the century, the German Jews were embarrassed by the clannish Yiddish speakers who strictly observed *kashruth* (dietary laws) and the Sabbath. Meanwhile, the wave of Yiddish speaking Jews generally criticized the German Jews as *"goyim"*.

The Gimbel's store that opened in Milwaukee in 1887 prospered. The trouble was that Adam Gimbel had seven sons and an eighth adopted one and he needed to expand the business to accommodate them. The saying was that Gimbel had a surplus of capital and a surplus of sons.

So he opened another store in Philadelphia at the 69th Street terminal area and eventually stores in downtown Pittsburgh and adjacent to the Herald Square terminal in New York City. The New York store's success was due to its multiple entrances from the terminal (though it eventually closed since those entrances and exits led to the highest shoplifting rate in the nation). That store's proximity to its major rival, Macy's, led to the saying "Does Macy's tell Gimbels?"

Philadelphia Gimbel Store in 1910

Eventually Gimbels acquired 36 department stores nationally and was the largest department store chain in the world. They bought out the Saks store on 34th Street where scenes were taken for the movie "Miracle on 34th Street' and then they opened a second store on Fifth Avenue, still known nationally as Saks Fifth Avenue. Presently Gimbels survives as the Boscov stores.

COLLEGE THESES

In 1978 I dug up my father, Joe Shulkin's, 1923 thesis "*__A History of the Development of Russian Pharmacy__*__*__" submitted for his B.S. in Pharmacy. The University of Wisconsin library keeps all theses on file in perpetuity, so I decided to also take a peek at the one I did in 1954 "*__The Quantitative Analysis of Anthranilic Acid in Human Urine__*__*__"

I thought that mine was a wonderful paper, an Opus Magnifico compared to his. Brilliantly conceived and executed, it was envied by all the big wigs in the Cancer Research Department, (though no one other than me had ever bothered to look it up).

Pop's thesis was hard to read, the ink having faded and paper yellowed during its 50 years imprisoned in a dusty box in the storage area. I just skimmed it. Wasn't all that important anyway. They didn't have antibiotics or anticancer drugs or even Botoxin for wrinkles back then, for God's sake.

Pop rambled on for 27 pages as to how pharmacology differed with the Russians depending upon whether they were Slavs, Poles, Teutonics, Estonians, Litvaks, Galician's, Georgians, Jews, or a dozen other brands I never heard of. It was comprehensive. He went back to prehistoric times with wizards, sorcerers and seers preparing potions, to Ivan the Great importing pill pushers from western Europe in 1324. The Czar opened the first public pharmacy in 1677 which was really a chemistry shop with interests in both mining and pharmaceutical gardens.

The Passport Laws of 1879 forbad Jews from owning pharmacies and those who did were to secure other management at once. Women pharmacists? Forget them. In 1900, they were not allowed to practice at all.

With the advent of communism, the government stopped discriminating but carefully controlled pharmacies and charged 10% of the business' gross as rent and it raised taxes at will, so that it hardly paid to run a drugstore. By 1920 there was such a scarcity of medicines such as acacia, sienna leaves, castor oil, gypsum .and narcotics that one had to buy them from soldiers who stole them from the army. Customers had to bring their own lard to have an ointment made.

"Pretty dull stuff compared to my anthranilic acid thesis!" I found myself saying aloud. But then again, Dad didn't have any schooling at all until he was 13 and he came to this country. He learned English and did grammar school, high school and college in just 10 years, often interrupting his studies to work helping support his father's large family.

Some paper mites and bookworms who had sampled both our theses, overheard me and one bookworm piped up,
"The father is twice as smart as the son!"
"Not so!" I found myself saying, "The father is ten times as smart".

Michael Tepper commented:
"Wow. I think frequently about how life is so much easier today. I am so aware at how much tougher life was then. But your father had an even tougher life than most. He faced persecution, the leaving home for a foreign country, and learning a new language, I'm sure the list goes on & on. I often think of my grandparents who made the same journey and had the same struggles – where would I be – literally – without the decisions they made (oy, Russia?)."

THE GALVESTON CONNECTION

My life partner, Sunny Shulkin, sometimes feels bombarded by too much information from my genealogic armory. So this story is about her father, Samuel Edelman, 1895-1981,

Samuel Edelman and Lillian Edelman

The Movement West

Sam was a foot soldier in the Jewish revolution of 1899 to 1914 when a million Jews emigrated mostly to the United States, changing forever the geographic, economic and even the religious nature of the Jewish people. There was a concerted effort by Jewish organizations to settle new immigrants like Sam west of the Mississippi River.

He had contracted with HIAS (The Hebrew Immigration Aid Society) while still in the old country to settle in Galveston or west of the Mississippi River in exchange for travel money to America. (He jokingly told me that another condition of his emigration was promising the Polish Government that he would never go back to Poland.)

There's a story, perhaps apocryphal, about his stopping in a Galveston bar for some *"schnapps"* as a 1911 immigrant. Hearing a voice call out "Are there any Jews here?", he trembled as he recalled the pogroms of his native Poland. But spotting him, the voice switched to Yiddish, *"Du bist a Yid?, kommt, dophin a minion."* (Are you Jewish?, Come, we need a minion).

There weren't all that many Jews in 1911 Galveston, so it was difficult observing religious ritual.

It was a bloodless revolution with a self selected army, but not a leaderless one. It was spearheaded, and the troops deployed, by wealthy German Jews who had come to America in the later 1800's and who, having thrived, had compassion for their Eastern European co-religionists but were opposed to their concentration in the New York area. The Jewish Colonization Association (ICA) founded by Baron Maurice de Hirsch had started sending Jews to Argentina back in 1891.

HIAS was not the only organization trying to enforce new Jewish immigration patterns in America. The Galveston plan was initiated by The Jewish Territorial Association (JTA) under the leadership of American banker Jacob Schiff, who was very concerned about the concentration of Jews (about 1.3 million by 1914) living in Manhattan- mostly on the poverty stricken and crime infested lower East Side. He correctly predicted that this would prompt the Government to restrict immigration from Eastern Europe as opposed to Western Europe, which had much larger quotas and fewer restrictions.

By 1905 The Industrial Removal Office (IRO) had funded 40,000 Jews to move to towns west of New York. The IRO president in London wanted to purchase land in the West which could become an autonomous Jewish Homeland though Schiff disagreed, feeling the land in the U.S. would shape the people rather than the people needing to shape the land.

At any rate, the agency carefully selected the people it funded for Galveston, choosing healthy single young men who had manual labor skills and excluding women and children under 16. They also needed to be affluent enough to pay for their own steamship ticket from Bremen, Germany to Galveston. This was a very different group than those who emigrated to Palestine, many of them family oriented religious people who wanted to die in a Jewish homeland, but who would have difficulty supporting themselves there.

Sam's History

Sam was the oldest son of his town's chief rabbi, Har Rev Eliezer Edelman, whose rabbinical tradition went back to Sam's namesake Rabbi Samuel Edelman, 1555-1631.

Certified as a "*shechet*" (the ritual slaughterer of chickens) Sam had come to Galveston hoping to work as a *shechet* but job opportunities for *shechets* were scarce in Texas. Finding it similar in Omaha, he then went to St. Paul, Minn., where his uncle, Rabbi Moses Edelman, was teaching Hebrew. (Moses was the grandfather of political activist Peter Edelman).

Fluent in Polish, Sam worked selling haberdashery to other Polish immigrants and on the store owner's retirement, he bought the store. He'd have stayed in St. Paul, except that in 1915 he was drafted into the First World War and sent to an army post in South Carolina for two years. The Army helped Sam assimilate and to Americanize and when he was discharged at Fort Dix, NJ, he bought a army surplus store with his savings

At a kosher restaurant in Asbury Park, NJ. he fell in love with a waitress, Lillian Popok. He married her and never left the East Coast after that. His was a passionate love and in 1975 he told me that he still remembered her phone number, Asbury Park 2893.

After operating a kosher delicatessen, they foresaw a new business opportunity, shoe rationing during WWII, and they operated Richards Shoes. It was a successful children's shoe store in suburban Philadelphia for 40 years.

Though HIAS, ITA, ICA, and the IRO all failed in their mission to keep Sam from settling east of the Mississippi, they had sponsored a person who contributed to the greatness of the U.S.

USOW vs. USOW

When my nephew, Robert Shulkin, was a student at the University of Pennsylvania Law School in 1975, he sent me a transcript of the first case in the Wisconsin State Supreme Court that involved a brother suing a brother. It was **Usow vs Usow et el**. It was decided on 12/5/1933 that my Dad's cousin Abe Usow owed his brother Joe Usow $90,000 because of some tricky stock transactions involving their partnership in The Badger Raincoat Company.

Abe Usow 1933

What the justices didn't know is that Abe Usow, 1882-1940, was really Eugene (Ushisoff} Usow and that his younger brother Eugene Usow was really Abe Usow. It was Eugene who owed Joe the money, not Abe.

What had happened was this. When the real Eugene left Russia in the early 1900's, he couldn't use his real name because he was avoiding conscription into the Russian Army. So he used his younger brother Abe's name. Some years later when the real Abe Usichisoff emigrated, and the Russo-Japanese War was over, he had to use his older brother's name because the Immigration people had him down as already having emigrated.

Once in America they couldn't go back to their real names since Eugene (now called Abe) had already established an identity here, drivers' license, bank loans, etc.

Note: One summer while at the University of Wisconsin in Madison, Jim Shulkin signed up to be called in for a summer job at the Miller Brewery in Milwaukee. But then he decided to go to summer school. When the brewery called to offer the job, Jim's brother Robert Shulkin answered the phone. Robert pretended to be Jim and took the job. He even passed for Jim at the pre-employment physical performed by his cousin, Dr. Abe Sverdlin.

Things got confusing at the end of the year when Jim got tax form 1099 for Robert's wages. Jim's accountant, brother-in law Michael Sattell, solved the problem in advising that IRS didn't care who paid as long as they got the money. Robert paid the tax as if he were Jim.

Mark Weiss Shulkin MD

ESTRANGEMENT IN THE FAMILY

The story of Joe Usow's son can now be told since all the persons involved are deceased. Joe's son was born in about 1930.

Horton Smith, who looked like Joe Usow with his barrel chest, round shoulders and stocky build, was an adopted child who in searching for his natural parents, found Joe Usow's name on his birth certificate. His biological mother was a school teacher back when school teachers couldn't be married since school boards reserved teaching jobs for single people who had to support themselves. He'd never met his real mother.

Growing up out west where non-Christians were considered foreigners, he traced his roots to Wausau, Wisconsin where he was warmly received by his cousin, Herbie Cohan. Horton looked forward to meeting his aunts and uncles and the family he'd never known but. However, Herbie's mother, Bernice Cohan, was not glad to see him. Bernice, a widow, had been left two and a half million by her single brother, Joe. She did not want to accept a slur on her brother's memory and perhaps was concerned that Horton might have a claim to the inheritance.

Horton made no formal claim to the money though it is said that he felt that his children deserved some small part of it. No one in the family ever heard from Horton again.

CHAPTER THREE
Between World Wars

THE INCIDENT AT MASSENA

Pogroms and official governmental persecution of the Jews may have been left behind in Polotsk, but anti-Semitism had not, and neither, it eventually transpired, had the infamous medieval shibboleth known as "The Blood Libel." This was the often church inspired practice of inciting riots by accusing Jews of having killed a Christian child in order to obtain blood for making *matzos.* They usually occurred around *Passover,* but in 1928, the day before *Yom Kippur,* an ugly echo of the old medieval blood libel was heard in Massena and this time Jake Shulkin played a central role.

A young Christian girl had disappeared shortly before dusk, and the word somehow spread that the Jews had killed her to get blood for the coming holy day. Willie Shulkin, Jake's oldest son, was interrogated, and because he suffered a mental aberration of some sort, seemed to confess to the crime. Later that day the rabbi was called to the police station for questioning, having run a gauntlet of an unfriendly, even menacing crowd, gathered outside the station. That evening the congregation banded together in the Synagogue basement fearing violence from angry townspeople.

Fortunately for the Jews of Massena, the little girl was found the next morning, having gotten lost in the woods behind her home. That did not end the matter for Uncle Jake, however. The man who had run away from a Russian army barracks was not about to be intimidated in the country he had worked so hard to reach. The full story is related in <u>Incident at Massena</u> by Saul Friedman, published by Stein and Day in 1978.

The essence of Jake's response is captured in the following excerpts from two letters he wrote: the first to Rabbi Stephen S. Wise, president of the American Jewish Congress, the other to Louis Marshall, president of the American Jewish Committee.

"Dear Dr. Wise:
We take the liberty of writing you of an unfortunate circumstance which occurred Sunday, *erev Yom Kippur.* On Saturday, September 22, a Christian child was lost. Sunday at noon, after an exhaustive search by the parents, police, firemen, and private citizens, there was still no trace of the child.

At about 12:30 p.m. a state trooper called our rabbi on the telephone. He instructed the rabbi to come to the police headquarters. He desired to have a conversation and obtain important information. Rev. Brennglass went as directed.

A mob had gathered in the police station. As the Rabbi entered there was an exclamation, 'Ah, here is Rabbi Brennglass.' A policeman called Rev. Brennglass into a private room and told him that a trooper would come in shortly. Within a few minutes the trooper came. The trooper asked the question, 'Do you know that a child has been lost?' Answer: 'Yes.' Question: 'Can you give any information if your people in the old country offer human sacrifices?' At this, Rabbi Brennglass immediately jumped at the trooper with the retort, 'I am surprised that an officer in the United States which is the most enlightened country in the world should dare to ask such a foolish and ridiculous question.'

The Rabbi then left the police station. His congregation gathered for *mincha* services and were told of the terrible situation. Each of the members of the small community was in a state of dispair [sic]. Each could imagine only the worst results because the excitement in the city was intense and each knew from history what the blood accusation had cost us

Sunday at 4:30 p.m. the child was found in the woods about one mile from her home. Now the rumor is broadcast that after the questioning of the Rabbi, the guilty became frightened and gave up the child.

We feel that we cannot drop this case. We are strong in our opinion that it is a national affair. We do not know how to proceed. We request that you immediately inform us what action to take."

After intervention by Wise and Marshall, and the notification of Governor Alfred E. Smith, those responsible for the incident were severely chastised and made to apologize to the Jewish community.

Jake wrote to Marshall, "We are glad to report to you that we were present at a hearing this morning on the recent incident which developed in our community. which hearing took place in the office of the Superintendent of the State Police. You will be informed of the action which has since been taken by the Superintendent, as reported by him, to the Governor of New York."

Jake was a Generous Man

The story doesn't fully present what Jake Shulkin really was to the rest of his large family. He had become wealthy and president of the Synagogue. A respected member of his community and true to both the letter and the spirit of Jewish law, he gave to those with less than he. Not only did he bring over sisters and brothers-in-law, but he continued to help those still in Russia. Believing his elder brother, Malech, to be in dire financial circumstances, Jake regularly sent money to him. When a nephew was without a job during the Depression, Jake provided a job and even a home.

KOSHER NOSTRA

If you've ever devised a scheme to avoid paying your library book fines or called an 800 number and threatened to cancel your credit card unless they forego the penalty for a late payment, you know that a criminal tendency runs in the family.

Zvi Hersh Shulkin

My Great Grandpa Zvi was arrested and sent to Vologda, Siberia from 1907 to 1910. The crime could have been bootlegging. Grandpa Zvi made his own whiskey and sold it in his home which was an inn, or a *"kretsma"*.

Zvi's son, my Grandpa Malech in Milwaukee, made bathtub whiskey and a great Passover wine which he supplied to the family and discreetly sold to members of his synagogue. Discreetly because the current liquor law allowed you to distill spirits only for your own use.

Malech Schulkin

The Jewish Mafiea

But Zvi's grandson, my cousin David Amdur, carried the family tradition to extreme. He was a "wise guy" in the Jewish Mafia, in the business of wholesaling Canadian hooch to retailers in Prohibition dry Cleveland. David's machinegun riddled body was found coiled in a roll of barbed wire fencing in 1931.

Left to right, David, Simon, Rose
and Mollie Amdur in a 1906 picture
.sent to Wolf Amdur in America

Yes, Virginia, there really was a Jewish Mafia. Prior to 1920 when Prohibition started, it was in the kosher chicken business. Hence it is nicknamed the "Kosher Nostra"

According to Sandy Sadowsky, in <u>My Life in the Jewish Mafia,</u>

"Among 6,000 New York area butchers who allegedly only sold kosher meat to fellow Jews, there were few who did not, at some point, deal in unkosher meat. The Jewish slaughterhouse system was also involved in price-fixing, extortion, racketeering, fist fights in the synagogue, and even murder. The intense rivalry and competition in the kosher poultry business, made it prey to racketeering and violence."

Actually the Jewish mafia preceded the Italian mafia. Gangstering is an immigration phenomenon and the Jewish wave of immigration came a decade earlier than the Italian's.

A Family Man

No one wants to hear that a Mafioso is a warm and kind hearted soul. That's not what sells newspapers. But David Amdur was.

When things got hot for him in Cleveland, either the police or other gangsters after him, David would lay low for a while visiting my parents in Milwaukee. They knew him to be pleasant and loving and he was fond of taking my brother, Dick, to the zoo or to the park. Other relatives were concerned about that and would ask my parents if they weren't concerned that he'd kidnap little Dickie. They weren't.

Back in the booming 20's the prohibition law was a very unpopular one. The police didn't bother enforcing the law as long as things were discreet and low key. Even my Dad, a pharmacist, kept a supply of Grandpa Malech's bathtub gin in his drug store safe, labeled "Spiritus Fermenti" with directions about its use "only for medicinal purposes".

JOSEPH SHULKIN 1950

The Amdurs settled in Gentile Sheboygan Wisconsin in 1907. David had come to America when he was five. Never a good student, he got into minor troubles in early adolescence. At 16 he ran away to join the Navy but the family hired detectives to find him and bring him home.

His father died in the Influenza epidemic when he was 17. That's when his mother, Rose Amdur, concerned that his older brother Simon Amdur, was too interested in the Christian girl next door, moved the family to Cleveland to live in a Jewish neighborhood and to be closer to her older sister Gussie Rosenberg (later changed to Weinstein).

Gussie had married a painter, David Rosenberg, who after being wanted by the New York City Police Department for selling stolen paint, changed his name to Weinstein and left town. Gussie divorced him and moved to Cleveland with her two kids in the early 20's. She made a good living making and selling Papa Zvi's "recipe" by the glass in her kitchen or in medicine bottles to take home. Later she bought a house in a better neighborhood but kept the old house just for business purposes.

She was the family matriarch, helping Malech and her other siblings out financially. The police knew about her operation but weren't about to keep a single old lady from supporting her family, so when they "knocked her over" every once and a while to make things look good, they gave her enough warning so the mash could be destroyed before the cops arrived.

David's first job was helping out his favorite aunt but before long he graduated to being a Mafia runner.

Things got competitive as the decade progressed and the Italian Mafia moved in. Loan sharking, gambling and prostitution were added to the product mix and the gangs began warring against each other. By 1930, Lucky Luciano was fighting an open battle for control of the Old Line Cosa Nostra. At a November 11, 1931 meeting, Meyer Lansky was able to unite Luciano's gang and the Jewish mobsters into a sophisticated coalition called the National Crime Syndicate, prompting Bugsy Siegel to say, "The Yids and the Dagos will no longer fight each other."

Jewish Business Genius

That was the Jewish forte', using intellectual skills to modernize and make a business more efficient. The Jews were the first ones to realize the link between organized crime and organized politics. They led the way in corrupting the police and city hall. They realized the value of gang syndicate cartels in business to reduce the killing of each other.

But they were too late to prevent David Amdur's assassination at the tender age of 29.

Note: It was the Russian custom to banish criminals and political activists to Siberia rather than send them to prison. Zvi took his wife and unmarried daughters with him and he prospered especially after the transcontinental railroad came through Vologda. He took in boarders and formed a *Shul* and had several business ventures going. In 1910, when his sentence was up, he asked permission to stay in Siberia. Russian authorities denied permission because Jews had to live within the pale.

It was the Jewish Mafia that had fixed the 1919 World Series or the Black Sox scandal. In the 1930s, Meyer Lansky and his gang stepped outside their usual criminal activities to break up rallies held by Nazi sympathizers, one in Yorkville, a German neighborhood in Manhattan. Lansky recalled,

"The stage in Yorkville was decorated with a swastika and a picture of Adolf Hitler. The speakers started ranting. There were only fifteen of us, but we went into action. We threw some of them out the windows. Most of the Nazis panicked and ran out. We chased them and beat them up. We wanted to show them that Jews would not always sit back and accept insults."

Sallyann Sack commented: "I don't think our great-grandfather was sent to Vologda for bootlegging. That got a much lesser punishment in czarist Russia. We have the words of one of our other cousins about this."

"I was told two competing stories. One is that some non-Jewish men who worked for Tzvi Hirsh came to him one winter to say that they were freezing and he, purportedly, replied, "Go cut some wood"–but the woods belonged to the Czar. When the men were caught and asked who told them they could cut wood in the czar's forest, they replied, "the Jew, Shulkin." The other story is murkier. Reportedly, Tzvi Hirsh had a feud with someone in the neighborhood and set fire to that person's barn–for which he was arrested and sent into exile–along with his minor children".

Mark Shulkin replied, "I agree about Tzvi. Also I wonder if *Tante* Gussie wasn't paying off the Cleveland police for their lenient treatment and if David didn't do some strong arm stuff. The Mafia wasn't looking for sweet soft hearted men."

Sallyann replied, "Yes, *Tante* Gussie did pay off the Cleveland police. My father told a great story about that. I haven't heard much about David except that he collected the "numbers" money for the gang—and was killed because he skimmed off some for himself.'

ANATOL SHULKIN

Daniel Shulkin of the Philadelphia Shulkins did a piece of Google research which showed Anatol Shulkin's name on a 1941 Mormon Church synagogue membership list. That led to Anatol Shulkin's connection to the family.

Anatol was born about 1900, the son of Abraham Shulkin who emigrated to Manhattan about 1908. A first child, he was named after his mother's side of the family which is why his name is of Belgian origin rather than Russian or Jewish.

His paintings of murals were political statements considered communistic before that was considered un-American. During the 1930's many Jewish liberals, including my father, Joe Shulkin, were opposed to the Spanish Dictator Franko during the Spanish revolution, favoring the left wing revolutionary forces.

The murals depict cultural incongruities while combining heroic scale, social conflict, and powerful design, boosting the popularity of murals in that era.

The privileged position that murals would claim over the decade was aided to a large degree by federally financed programs offering relief to unemployed artists while securing decoration for the walls of public buildings. Anatol Shulkin's commission, however, fell outside that network of government patronage.

The main dining room of Manhattan's Barbizon-Plaza Hotel at 106 Central Park South, erected in 1930, was the seemingly unlikely backdrop for Anatol's American Life mural. Although the specific circumstances of this 28 foot mural's arrival within the establishment's stylish Art Deco interior are unrecorded, its placement may be attributable to the hotel's receptivity to contemporary art, inferred by its billing as New York's "first fully equipped music-artist residence center," complete with two concert auditoriums, a library, art studios, and exhibition rooms catering to creative tenants.

The mural's installation at the Barbizon-Plaza in 1934 coincided with Anatol Shulkin's own residency there. More significant was the Barbizon-Plaza's concurrent serving as host to An American Group, an organization activated in 1931 to arrange show space for "individualistic" artwork with "something to say" and consequently foreclosed from traditional gallery venues. The hotel facilitated exhibitions for the group for three seasons before its members opted to turn their programs over to professional gallery management.

The provocative mood of Shulkin's mural, though not necessarily suited to whetting patron's appetites, apparently was more tolerable for a hotel than that of the American Group artists, to whom uncensored expression was paramount.

For his grand opus, Shulkin marshaled figures and symbols that embodied the polymorphic culture of Depression-era New York. These he welded into a dense, rhythmical design that delivers a cumulative portrait of the decadence, confusion, and economic and racial strains afflicting the city.

The FUGU Plan

I'll always remember December 7, 1941. On that Sunday afternoon I was sitting in a movie theatre when the screen went blank and it was announced that the Japanese had bombed Pearl Harbor and that President Roosevelt had declared war upon Japan. As a 12 year old, I didn't know the significance of the event or that about 20 young men on my family tree would eventually be listed as deceased between 1941 and 1945. I would have been particularly astounded to hear that the Japanese government had been repatriating Jewish victims of Nazi persecution for years during which time America had closed its borders to them.

Two decades later, while gathering family history from my wife Sunny's parents, I learned that Sunny's Dad's younger brothers in New York, Harry and Saul Edelman, had been rescued from the Nazis by the Japanese. They had been "*yeshiva buchers*" at the Rabbinical Seminary in Mir, a Polish city prior to the Russian invasion of Poland in September 1939. (Mir was occupied by the Germans when they invaded Russia on June 21, 1941. Now it's in Belarus).

The Plan to Industrialize China

This story is detailed in <u>Desperate Voyagers- The Fugu Plan</u> by Rabbi Marvin Tokayer and Mary Swartz published in 1979 and still available on Amazon. com. Fugu is the Japanese word for poisonous and the name the Japanese give to the puffer fish which if prepared properly is a delicacy but if poorly prepared is poisonous. The name Fugu Plan portrays well the Japanese ambivalence about Jews at a time when the Japanese were still isolated from other cultures.

Influenced by large loans from American Jewish banker Jacob Shiff in 1900 which insured their victory in the Russo-Japanese War, the Japanese believed that Jews were powerful and wealthy and that International Jewry could be an important ally.

They admired Judaism and seeing theoretical similarities to Shintoism they established some Jewish synagogues in Japan proper. But after <u>The Protocols of the Elders of Zion</u>, an anti-Semitic mis-description of the power of world Jewry and its wealth, was translated into Japanese, they also believed that Jews could dominate the governments of the countries that they lived in and they regarded Jews as potentially dangerous.

During their 1930's decade long war with China, Japan re-settled tens of thousands of Jewish refugees into Japanese occupied China (Manchuria and Shanghai for example). They expected that the Jewish international bankers, like the Rothschilds, would support their co-religionists financially and that they would industrialize the settlements. The Japanese especially hoped to win the political favor of American Jews, encouraging their economic investments in Japanese territories.

The Japanese discontinued these relationships with the Jewish people in 1939, however, when they entered into "The Tripartite Alliance" with Germany and Italy. To their credit, however, they refused the Nazi edict to euthanize the Jewish community in Shanghai during World War II, instead limiting the Jew's civil rights and their freedom to travel.

The Escape from Russia

No one in the Russian occupied Polish territory (within the Pale) was allowed a passport, making escape from the impending German invasion of the area impossible.* The Japanese Vice Consul, Chiune Sugihara, appealed to his superiors in Japan for permission to issue transit visas for Jews to leave for Japan but his requests were repeatedly denied. In issuing these visas to the entire Yeshiva student body and to 6000 others anyway, he sacrificed his diplomatic career and risked his and his family's life. **

The plan was that the Yeshiva students would take the Trans Asiatic Railway to Vladiovostek, travel by ship for a short stay in Japan and then proceed to Curacao in the Dutch West Indies. Curacao had not yet formalized immigration regulations and did not require entrance visas.

Predictably Japan did not allow them to enter Japan. Before the students could get to Curacao the Germans had invaded Holland and the newly appointed Nazi Governor General of Curacao denied them entry. For a year the ship sailed from port to port, taking on food and water but it was not allowed to disembark its passengers. The students were literally men without a country.

Family Relationships

When my wife, Sunny, was five in 1941, her mother traveled to Washington to successfully lobby her congressmen for legislation that allowed her brothers-in-law to enter the then isolationist United States. Sunny remembers enjoying her two adoring young uncles when they briefly lived with her family in Philadelphia. The uncles left Philadelphia because Harry felt that Sunny's family, though observant, was not strict enough in living up to religious traditions.

Harry eventually became a rabbi in Brooklyn and Saul settled in Far Rockaway, New York, where he was a *moel,* performing ritual circumcisions.

Harry's son was dwarfed because of taking steroids to treat juvenile arthritis. The Philadelphia family arranged to collect cadaver pituitary glands from area hospital morgues for him. Human growth hormone, which had not at the time been synthesizable, was extracted from the glands and the child was able to grow just tall enough to be able to use a public phone. (Never married, he devoted his life to caring for Harry in his old age.)

Though the families stayed in contact over the years, the New York families did not attend Sunny's and my wedding because the food would not be kosher enough. But Sunny and I had the unique experience of attending Saul's daughter's strictly Orthodox wedding in Far Rockaway. (Saul's daughter then emigrated to Israel.)

These cordial relations were strained in 1981 when Rabbi Harry unexpectedly came to Sunny's father, Sam Edelman's, funeral. He took over officiating it and in his sermon he admonished the family to donate lots of money to charity in Sam's name because Sam had not been sufficiently observant of Jewish law to be able to get into Heaven.

Notes: * **Yocheved Dynovsky–Brisnansky of Hadera, Israel** (Sam Edelman's cousin) **related:** "I'd heard from Christians who witnessed Sunny's grandfather, Har Rav Eliezer Edelman, Chief Rabbi of Rubiezewiscze, Poland's march to the center of the town in 1944 where he was shot to death by Nazi soldiers. He'd volunteered to be executed in exchange for sparing some 900 other Jewish lives. She wrote,

"He was wrapped in his *Talit* and wearing his *Tfilin*. He was accompanied by Rabbi Gedaliah Tzofin on one side and by a Mr. Eisenbook, the secular head of the town, on the other. The men walked standing erect with their heads high. His wife, Rachel Edelman, went to her death with similar dignity, perhaps with her ready smile. There was no screaming, no tears, no pleading for mercy. They were living out their Jewish destiny. They knew they were dying the death of martyrs."

** Vice Consul Sugihara was honored by the State of Israel in 1985 with the Righteous Among Nations award for his humanitarianism.

*** I heard a story, perhaps apocryphal, that an American soldier of Jewish faith, feeling homesick in post war American occupied Japan, attended a Sabbath service in a synagogue there. After the service he approached the Rabbi to tell him how much he enjoyed the service. The Rabbi, observing the soldier's pale complexion and horizontal eyes, said in broken English, "Funny, you no looking Jewish."

Nedra Fetterman commented, "I empathize with my Grand Uncle Harry who only wanted to save his brother's soul in getting him into Heaven".

Reply: Samuel Edelman did indeed get into Heaven. He has a place right next to God reserved for those who had a particularly hard time getting there. Perhaps he had a hard time getting there because of a curse. During the Great Depression, Sam got letters from his sister in Vilna, either Sarah or Bella, announcing the birth of her children. He acknowledged the "*simchas*" with cash gifts which he could ill afford. But as the birth announcements began to come more and more frequently, Sam realized that they were a money raising scam and he stopped sending money. His sister, angry about his lack of generosity, put a curse on him.

Hyman Edelman wrote in 1981,"Enclosed is some correspondence with the director of the YIVO Institute Library in Manhattan discussing his continuing dialogue with Harry Edelman about the appropriateness of using my $5000.00 donation to establish a memorial to our martyred father Har Rev Eliezer at YIVO."
Comment: The Edelmans were Ultra-Orthodox Haridim and Harry felt YIVO was too liberal to honor his father's role in Jewish history.

The family tree lists a woman born about 1550 named Edel –the Yiddish diminutive for Edith- whose son-in-law, honoring her for supporting his study of Torah, took the surname Edelsman. (Rabbis took surnames because of their need to identify their publications centuries before other Jews, who feared military conscription and taxes in doing so.)

OVERSIGHT ON MACKINAC ISLAND

During the summer of 1963, Dick, Sydelle, Mark, Sunny and all their children and their children's Shulkin grandparents, vacationed for a week on Mackinac Island off the coast of Lake Michigan. No cars were allowed on the island and there was no bridge to the mainland. The only way to reach it was by a large ferryboat.

Top: Dick, Sydelle, Sunny, Nedra, Jim, Marion, and Mark Shulkin
Bottom: Bob Shulkin, Lisa Sattell, Dara Aronoff,
David Shulkin and Joseph Fetterman in 1980

We practically took over the hotel with 12 people all named Shulkin. It was a hectic week for the young mothers with six kids between them to manage. The challenge was organizing everybody to get ready for group activities. The children were quite young; Dara - 11, Bob and Nedra - 8, Jimmy - 6, David and Lisa - not yet 5.

It was grandparent Heaven having all the children together, but grandparents weren't responsible for keeping track of them and all the luggage and paraphernalia that went along with them, the most valuable of which was Dara's guitar.

The day of departure was particularly challenging because we had to be sure to get everybody together for the trip to the ferry dock. The ferry only left once a day. Sydelle assigned Jimmy to sit on the hotel porch guarding Dara's guitar, while she and the adults attended to luggage and the usual details involved in leaving a vacation spot.

We made the ferry on time and we were a half hour out on the water, pleased with ourselves for a very successful vacation. Then Sydelle Shulkin, the heroine of this story, noticed that Jimmy was missing.

Sydelle was frantic! She tearfully appealed to the captain, apparently an empathetic man. He turned the ferryboat around and returned us and about 50 other passengers back to the island. When we got to the hotel, there was Jimmy, calmly still guarding the guitar, as if nothing unusual had happened.

FAMILY WAR HEROES

As you climb our family tree, at every branch you'll find young men who died in the first half of the 1940's. Most of them are war heroes who did not live long enough to be acknowledged by posterity for having sacrificed their lives for their country.

Some of them, had they lived, would have gone on to have distinguished military careers such as did Col. I. A. Shulkin, 1928-2007, the son of Abraham Shulkin, the Sioux City woodcarver. He'd fought in WW II and Korea and then was the Liaison Officer to NATO.

Another still surviving family war hero is Sunny Shulkin's first cousin Major General Stanley Hyman, who fought in Korea and Vietnam winning the Distinguished Service Medal, the Legion of Merit with Two Oak Leaf Cluster, the Defense Meritorious Service Medal, theDepartment of the Army Staff Badge and the Organization of the Joint Chief's of Staff Badge.

A book about family who died defending their country would begin with the story of Lt.Ben Ghetzler, 1906-1941.

He was of the Rosen/Shulkin/Zimmermann branch, his life reconstructed by his nephew Dick Zimmerman on http://www. online-literature.com/forums/showthread.php?t=31803.

Typical of first generation Americans, Ben was dual-cultured. His loyalties were to family, country, Navy and God, in that order. The first of 11 siblings to graduate high school, he enlisted in the Navy in 1925. After boot camp at Great Lakes and a tour on a west coast destroyer, he'd distinguished himself enough to be appointed to the Naval Academy at Annapolis Officer Training class of 1931.

What '*nachus*' for his immigrant family back in San Antonio!

After graduation, as an Ensign and Assistant Turret Officer on the Battleship Colorado, he loved seeing the world on peacetime duty. In 1933, he was assigned Communications' Officer on a gunboat protecting merchant vessels on the Yangzte River in China. By 1935, he was the Engineering Officer on the USS Omaha touring the East coast and Europe.

But when Germany over ran Europe and began the extermination of Jews in 1938, his greatest wish was for the then isolationist U.S. to enter the fray directly. It already did a minor role in supplying munitions and other resources to the Allies. He wanted to see action. That's the way Americans with dual loyalties to their culture and their country felt.

In May 1941, he was assigned to the destroyer Reuben James with the understanding that after six months he would assume its command. The ship, part of a convoy from Argentia, Newfoundland, was going to Iceland, where it was to turn the British merchant vessel it was protecting from submarines over to the Royal Navy. Unfortunately, it was torpedoed by a German U-boat on October 31, 1941.

The Reuben James was the first U.S. vessel sunk by enemy action and it was only ten weeks prior to the attack on Pearl Harbor. The forward section, where the officers were, sank immediately and Ben, who'd been scheduled to take command of the ship on completion of that mission, went down with his ship.

CHAPTER FOUR

Second Half of the 20th Century

HYPERTROPHIC PYLORIC STENOSIS

Lillian Edelman (1901—1992) as a young woman.

Lillian Edelman wrote the following letter to her daughter, Sunny, on March 11, 1954, four months to the day before Sunny's and my wedding. Sunny was a freshman at the University of Wisconsin 800 miles away. I was a medical student at UW. Lillian and I hadn't met yet, so her sentiments were more about doctors generally than about me.

"You really haven't had the chance to know Mark too well, so believe me, when I say that you can go out years, and still not really know a person. Don't let me persuade you one way or another, but if you are looking for someone with a lot of humor and fun, I don't think you will find it in an M.D. because to be a really good doctor it takes a rather mature young man and they see and go thru so much that the tension subdues their real self.

"Life is a long stretch and it's best to plan for the long pull, not just for the few years you are going through now. Please Sonya, don't take this that I am not talking up Mark, it's not that at all. It's just this, if you feel he is Mr. Right then face it, but remember it means the rest of your life and if you feel otherwise, face that also.

"Every girl feels that maybe I ought to wait, maybe I should look around more,"

If I had taken her comments personally, it would have been because I didn't know a piece of Lillian's past history.

A Child Is Ill

In 1921, Lillian gave birth to a son, Jerome Edelman, nicknamed Sonny. He was born with Hypertrophic Pyloric Stenosis, a rare congenital disorder. It runs in Jewish families, especially in males. It's a narrowing of the exit to the stomach that prevents food from flowing into the small intestine to be digested.

So Sonny from birth vomited undigested milk while remaining hungry and crying for food. There was no adequate medical treatment at the time. He failed to gain weight and keeping him hydrated and replacing the chlorides lost in his vomiting would despair anyone, let alone an oldest sister, like Lillian, programmed to take care of children. At six months, Sonny was withering away.

Lillian heard about a pediatric surgeon in New York City who was doing the newly discovered Feder-Ramstedt operation that cured the condition. It involved splitting the pyloric muscle at the exit of the stomach while not breaking into the stomach's lining. Delicate surgery, no one else in the eastern United States could do it.

She traveled the 100 miles from Philadelphia to New York with the sick child. The famous doctor had set his fee at $5000.00 and he insisted it be paid prior to his doing the surgery. This was 35 years before the birth of Blue Cross and Lillian had no money. But she'd have promised anything and she agreed to meet the doctor in the hospital lobby to give him the cash just before surgery.

The next morning she hid behind a pillar as she watched the surgeon waiting to get his money and then, as expected, leave to do the scheduled surgery without it.

Silent Grief

The operation was successful but the patient died the next day. It hadn't been possible to restore the child's fluid and electrolyte balance.

Lillian never spoke of Sonny to anyone after that. She bore her grief in silence.

The exception was that once a year on the anniversary of Sonny's death, his *Jahrzeit*, she'd spend the whole day in Sonny's room, crying.

That's the way it was with that generation. My parents and grandparents never spoke of the Old Country and the loved ones they left behind. Such memories open up a floodgate of sadness too difficult to bear. The problem with avoiding the mourning process that way is that the mental energy required for such repression is then not available for more productive use. It struggles to get free and it commonly does so only once a year on the *jahrzeit*.

Was it just coincidence that when it was Lillian's turn to name her third child, she chose the name, Sonya or was she unconsciously replacing Sonny?*

Was it unconscious motivation that prompted Sonya to write a poem about wanting to be a surgeon,** and at age 13, to change her name to "Sunny"?. Lillian was upset about the name change and in the discussion about it that followed the story about Sonny's death came to the surface.

The day of mourning each year stopped after that. What hadn't stopped, at least at the time of the letter, was Lillian's feeling about doctors.

Notes:
* In the Jewish tradition, the wife names the first child, the husband the second and the wife names the third.

**Sunny's poem:

<u>GROWING PAINS</u>
When I grow up (although I'm three)
A famous surgeon I shall be.
But then I thought of fame in war
(I must decide before I'm four).

I see me now as president
But of that job I'm hesitant.
I must admit that it'd be heaven
But that's for old ones almost seven.

It's been rumored I can act
I have talent, that's a fact.
I'd better end– my piece I've said.
Another reason, it's time for bed.

ANTI-SEMITISM IN AMERICA

Anti-Semitism has been around for over 2000 years, beginning with the teachings of both the Catholic and Protestant churches that Jews were responsible for Christ's death. There was some relief from it with the age of enlightenment but as Europe became more divided into national world powers, anti-Semitism thrived as a political issue. Well-known examples were the pogroms in Russia and the famous Dreyfus case in 1896 France.

The mostly German Jews who came to America in the late 1800s, before the mass immigration of the early 20th century, had little difficulty assimilating and were often accepted as leaders of their communities. However Russian immigrants brought their plague with them to the New World. The German Jews, already Americanized, were embarrassed by their clannishness and isolation, and their strict observance of orthodox religious traditions. German Jews, though charitable as a group, were not sympathetic to the immigrants as individuals. They were often the owners of clothing factories and other business who treated the Russian Jews as cheap labor to be exploited. Intermarriage between the two groups was frowned upon.

Ulysses S. Grant

In America, General Ulysses S. Grant expelled Jews from his army and from a newly conquered territory in Tennessee but only out of ignorance. His military order 100 was quickly over ruled as unconstitutional by President Lincoln.

The circumstances were that Jews were on both sides of the Civil War including some Jewish cotton plantation owners who favored slavery. Clothing manufacturers in the Northeast required cotton from the South to fabricate tents and uniforms for the union army leading to unusual trade agreements for warring sections of a country. That created a black market in cotton with price increases to "what the traffic would bear". General Grant was in the position of having to issue permits for the sale of cotton to the enemy plantation owners, some of whom were Jewish.

Though a courageous military hero, he was a naïve personality who felt that people generally were honest and kind and that money gouging Jews were causing his military supply problems. Grant's naïveté' explained not only his uncharacteristic military order but the financial corruption later in

63

his presidential administration when only his appointed administrators and not he personally were found guilty of fraud. Grant was not anti-Semitic as president and he had the popular support of the Jewish electorate.

Henry Ford

Popular as a "good old boy" for his accomplishments in the auto industry, Henry Ford was an adamant anti-Semite all his life. He believed the misrepresentations of Judaism in the "forged" translations of The Protocols of Zion and he was outspoken in his prejudices. He published The International Jew, The World's Foremost Problem in 1915.

On June 16, 1916, the Chicago Tribune published an editorial describing Ford as an "ignorant idealist, cheap and vulgar, and an anarchist enemy of the United States so incapable of thought that he cannot see the ignominy of his own performance." Ford sued the Tribune for libel.

He proved the Tribune correct in their assessment of him during six days of his being cross examined on the witness stand by the Tribune's lawyer.

Question: Has there ever been a revolution in the United States?
Ford: I think I heard there was.
Question When?
Ford: About 1812.
Question: Who was Benedict Arnold?
Ford: I think I've heard the name but I can't place him. Maybe he's a writer!

Strangely Ford won the libel suit though he was awarded only $.06 instead of the millions he sued for.

He did issue an apology for some of his statements but he continued his fascist rhetoric to the point that Hitler gave him an award. In order that his views not be distorted, he bought a newspaper, the Dearborn Independent.

The paper had only .009% street sales. By Ford's executive order each Ford dealership had a quota of subscriptions they had to sell. Some dealers gave away subscriptions; others included them in the price of car sales. Some Jewish dealers gave up their dealerships rather than comply.

Isolationism Stimulates Prejudice

Hitler's coming to power in 1933 evoked the family's empathy for their German co-religionists but they remained silent publicly for fear of evoking more anti-Semitism in their own country. My father was particularly offended by Charles Lindberg, who had the applause of the enemies of the United States throughout the world.

A Belgian businessman, a devout "collaborationist" with the Nazis, said during WWII, "Lindbergh will be the next President of the United States. He could get along splendidly with Hitler. We are all for him."

Whether Lindbergh welcomed it or not, he had the enthusiastic applause of the Nazi Bund, the Fascist societies, and of all the most violently antidemocratic groups in this country, from the followers of Father Coughlin to the most eccentric Kluxer. As President of the America First Committee he had often expressed antiJewish beliefs which he attributed to causing the Great Depression, unemployment, and Americans getting into the war in Europe. To his credit, as president of the committee, he later recanted his anti-Semitic remarks and to his credit he expelled Henry Ford and Father Charles Coughlin from the organization for similar remarks.

Coughlin was a Catholic priest who had a "Fire and Brimstone" weekly radio show that 30% of Americans listened to faithfully. After the 1929 crash, he switched to becoming a monetary reform activist who blamed Jewish international bankers for the Depression. His speeches were anti -government generally and he spoke of Franklin "D"oublecross Roosevelt. By 1940 both Roosevelt and the Catholic church had banned him from radio and he went back to being a parish priest.

America entering the war softened the public anti-Semitic sympathies, though I remember the German American Bund having referred to "President Rosenfeld and his Jew Deal." It was still active in Milwaukee during early WWII.

More personal experience with anti-Semitism included applying to only the State of Wisconsin medical school in 1949 because private medical schools and out of state schools had quotas for Jewish applicants. In 1960, real estate agents would not show me properties in Gentile "gentleman's agreement restricted" neighborhoods and travel agents openly told me which hotels would not accept reservations if one's name sounded Jewish. When I was interviewed for staff privileges at the Institute of the Pennsylvania Hospital, I was told that I'd be more comfortable on the staff of a Jewish Federation sponsored hospital. I was!

SOUTH STREET

I remember South Street when visiting relatives both as a teenager and after having moved to Philadelphia in 1960. It was, and still is, a Greenwich Village or Soho experience frequented now by new agers socializing on weekend evenings and Sunday afternoons.

Back then there were street musicians, clowns and magicians performing for whatever you cared to contribute. There were kosher restaurants including Levis' kosher hotdog stand with an unforgettable fat juicy wiener and there were a gaggle of shoe and clothing stores. People overflowed the sidewalks, ambling down the center of the one way street giving way to slow moving automobiles and mounted policemen.

Mostly I remember walking past the men's clothing stores where a "barker" or "puller-in" would touch my sleeve and soto voco in Yiddish, "Come inside, You can get a bargain". (*"Cummen Sie arien. Du kennst a bargain kreigen)"*

And you could. Especially if you were the first customer of the day and the haggle factor favored the customer. Size wasn't the salesman's concern. Every suit looked "just great on you". It always "fit perfectly" and besides that the alterations were free of charge.

"All the doctors and lawyers are wearing this suit", claimed the salesman.

Prices were negotiable and until the price was agreed upon, you doubted that you wanted that suit and you had serious misgivings about whether your wife would like it.

Cousin Dick Zimmerman shares a story about a "hearing impaired" suit salesman. He yells out to the shop owner, "How much for this suit?"

"Twenty nine dollars!" the proprietor shouts back.

"How much?"

"Twenty nine! Ni*ne and twantzig*!"

"I can't hear you!"

"Two, nine, for God's sake!" screams the boss.

The salesman turns to the customer and says "It's $19.00." The customer quickly buys the suit, though he may be overpaying a few dollars.

Was it a re-creation of old world Polotsk?

Note: South Street hasn't changed all that much 50 years later, except that the street is now closed to traffic and the policemen walk their beat in pairs. The small shops are more of a mix of tattoo parlors and astrology readers, electronic discounters, and upscale restaurants along with cheese steak and hoagie* stands detectable a block away by tempting aromas.

ATLANTIC CITY

I spent hot summer weekends in my early years in Milwaukee at Bradford Beach on the Lake Michigan shore. I never saw the ocean until 1946 when I was 17. I visited my grand aunt, Yetta Benn, in Philadelphia. Philadelphia folks always take visiting relatives to Atlantic City to see the Ocean. That's how I discovered the old, now almost forgotten, Atlantic City.

I was amazed that the streets had been named after the squares on my Monopoly game board, or perhaps it was vice versa. It was a swinging place back then before the advent of the casinos in the 1970's destroyed its luster.

In Margate, I met and fell in love with Lucy the elephant. She was almost 50 years older than I, having been born in 1882, the brainchild of a real estate developer who was issued a patent for her so that no one else could ever build an animal building. During the Victorian era she was an architectural wonder having been crafted out of curved wood and sheets of hammered tin. Lucy was large enough to be seen from eight miles out at sea. Initially a hotel, she became a bar except during prohibition from 1920 to 1933.

Atlantic City had been slowly dying since the 1960's. Legalizing gambling there was an ill-fated attempt to revive it. It was succumbing to the advent of the automobile and expressways which made daytrips more convenient than renting or buying a vacation house there for longer stays.

Steel Pier boasted rides for kids, several movie theatres and varied inexpensive restaurants. Live entertainers were featured, including a lady who every hour on the hour dove off the pier into the ocean on horseback. You could spend the day just on Steel Pier. It closed down some years later as the tourist business slowed.

Lucy also succumbed to the drop in tourism and was in such disrepair that she'd been condemned as a safety hazard. Happily, before she could be demolished, the city of Margate took her over in the late 70's and she's been restored as a $4.00 a ticket tourist attraction.

In spite of a cool breeze off the shore, Atlantic City was hot and humid in August so we found relief sitting in the air conditioned, easy chaired lobbies of luxury hotels such as the Shelbourne, the Traymore, and the Claridge, which have all given way to modern casino hotels.

Also gone are the stately homes along the Boardwalk built by wealthy Atlantic City early settlers. Some of them succumbed to subdivision into small apartments or elder care homes prior to being purchased by the casinos. I remember heart rendering stories of elderly residents still living in them who refused to sell to the casinos at any price. The casinos then built themselves around and on top of those homes until their owners died off.

Plying the Boardwalk was a flotilla of wicker stroller chairs, foot-powered by their owners who negotiated for their services by the hour or by the trip.

Bicycle and roller skate rental shops came up every few blocks. Outdoor booths vended souvenirs, cotton candy, salt water taffy, ice cream and ears of corn on a stick. Levis had a New York style kosher hot dog stand. Captain Starns was the best known sea food restaurant in the area but I liked the all-you-can-eat smorgasbord at Zaberers better. There were also movie theatres, art galleries and upscale clothing and furniture stores.

Both sides of the boardwalk were lined with the "home base" benches of elderly people who met their friends and relatives there each weekend. The younger guys and the chicks promenaded the length of the boardwalk in their Sunday finest in search of meeting each other. There were outdoor stands of pitchmen demonstrating new kitchen gadgets with clever patter that always drew a crowd.

But best of all were the auctions. You'd sit on folding chairs in a small audience that kept enlarging as low priced items sold off for peanuts. A genuine leather billfold went for a dollar or a table lamp for two dollars. Everything going cheap enough to get a crowd into their seats. Some of the audience were *shills* but no one could guess which ones.

While the auctioneer was warbling off knick-knacks at reasonable prices, the *shills* were silent. Then when the room was full, and after announcing that dealers were not welcome to bid, the auctioneer would begin with "flawless" blue white diamond necklaces that you could try on for close inspection or zircon engagement rings "indistinguishable" from real diamond ones.

The bids started out low, increasing with claims about the size and quality of the gems and also with the number of *shnooks* and *shills* bidding them up.

Though Sunny and I hadn't come looking to buy jewelry, the crowd's enthusiasm was contagious. We knew that most of the action came from *shills* and only a little from the *shnooks* but we left feeling that maybe if we'd gotten into the bidding we could have scored a pair of earrings or a "diamond" necklace on the cheap.

THE GIFT

Watching a re-run of "Pretty Woman" with Richard Gere and Julie Roberts, I noticed a scene at Barbara's Quickie Grill with its 57 year old Afro-American proprietor standing in the background with a knowing look.

This bit part player was Barbara Knox. Her facial expression seemed to me all about her identification with Julie Roberts in having had received a gift from a generous man. The man was Louis Shulkin, son of Abraham (the famous woodcarver) and his second wife Yoche, and father of Michael D. Shulkin (who was in the computer software business in California) and his daughter, Audrey Shulkin.

I'd read in the Los Angeles times in 1987 that Louis and his wife Anita retired from running Lou's Quickie Grill and signed the business over to Barbara who had worked for them as a waitress/cook for 33 years. Barbara was 57 at the time. Here's a quote from the LA Times.

OBITUARY/ Barbara Knox, 1933 - 2008
(January 12, 2008 by Valerie J. Nelson, Times staff writer)

When the Shulkins told Barbara Knox they were going to sign the restaurant over to her, "It was like a dream come true," she said in 1987.

"I started praying every night: 'Lord, make it true, grant me the Quickie Grill.'" Yet she worried, "I didn't think I could make it. I thought, 'When Lou leaves, the customers will leave.'"

THE CIRCUMCISION

It was May 1955, I'd just graduated medical school and I was doing my year of internship at Mount Sinai Hospital of Milwaukee. I was born there 25 years earlier and I got to work alongside the nurse who assisted in my birth. My brother Dick was born there too. We all had good feelings about "our" Hospital.

It was like family. It wasn't prestigious academically and it didn't pay me a living wage ($200.00/month) but our medical and hospital care was free. Sunny was pregnant and our daughter Nedra was born there that month and then nine days later Dick's wife Sydelle gave birth to their first son, Robert. We loved our hospital.

Well, we loved it until a few days after Robert's birth when Sydelle found out that he'd been mistakenly circumcised along with the Gentile babies even though his ritual *bris (Brit Milah/circumcision ceremony)* was still some days off. The Hospital's *moel* was deviously planning to substitute another baby for the ceremony, thinking that we wouldn't know the difference. After all don't all babies look the same?

We felt betrayed!

What's more my Grandpa Malech Shulkin was president of the very orthodox *Leibovatcher Shul* and he took circumcisions seriously. Malech worried that Robert, if not circumcised according to strict tradition, would be a *shagitz*.

Dick conferred with Rabbi Twersky, the most orthodox of the orthodox Hassidic rabbis in Milwaukee for advice. Rabbi Twersky had no precedent for this situation but the rabbi had a reputation as a peace maker.

He put orthodoxy aside, giving thought to the mother's feelings as well as the great grandfather's and to the moel's. His solution, was in the spirit of ancient Jewish tradition as defined in Rabbi Hillel's (110 BCE-10 CE) precursor of the Golden Rule, which stated

"If I am not for myself who will be for me?
If I am for myself who am I?
And if not now — WHEN?"

The Rabbi ruled that Robert having been circumcised by a Jewish pediatrician of good moral character in the hospital nursery could have a legitimate *Bris* ceremony conducted by the *moel* later.

Sydelle Shulkin commented, "Actually, Mark, The *moel* Dick hired had circumcised Robert by mistake at the circumcision ceremony of another Jewish couple's son that morning, one day prior to Robert's ceremony."

CHAPTER FIVE

Personal Stories

THE HOSTAGE

During the 1979 Iranian revolution, students took over the American Embassy in Tehran holding 52 American officials hostage for 444 days from November 4, 1979 until to Jan 20, 1981 just moments after President Reagan took office.

So I get this letter from Milt Gelman, the Hollywood film and TV script writer who is smelling a story to write.

"April 29, 1980
From: Cuzzin Milt
To: Cuzzin Mark

I have a most important request. A letter came that one of our relatives is a hostage. For reasons I cannot discuss it is imperative that I know the name. I am in the middle of something that deals directly with an outside hope that, if certain specifics happen, my mentioning that name of someone closely connected to me will give that person special protection and consideration. I guarantee that the name will never be spoken unless and until that situation arises. I pledge absolute secrecy, but please I beg of you let me know who that hostage is. It could very well be a potentially important safety factor. I cannot say any more. If you will be good enough to trust me, it might help that person.

Enough already. Bless you, you rotten little kid."

I replied after the hostages release.

"To: Cuzzin Milt
From: Cuzzin Mark

He is John Limbert, Ph.D, born 3/10/43. John is retired now and lives with his Iranian wife, Parvenah in Vermont. They have two grown children Mandana, 41, and Shervin, 39.

The reason I didn't tell you back then isn't that I didn't believe you or trust in you, but because he was in such danger. They were kept incommunicado in the dark, subjected to beatings, forced confessions and mock executions with automatic weapons held to their heads. They were blindfolded and frequently moved from place to place. They were the first victims of a modern state sponsored terrorism.

Fluent in Farsi as the group's negotiator, along with being Jewish and having in-laws and many upper class social connections in Tehran, John was particularly suspect as an enemy of the Revolution. John's wife and two small kids (and his parents) were also in danger.

The Limberts were especially shocked at the unexpected nature of Iranian hostility toward them, John had lived in Tehran as an adolescent while his parents worked there as US AID officials. John spent two years in the Peace Corps there where he met his wife and they married in 1966. He taught English for seven years at Shiraz University and he joined the Foreign Service in 1973. He had only been assigned to the US embassy in Iran for 12 weeks when the students overran it."

Notes: The U.S. embassy had been overrun when President Carter granted the deposed Shah of Iran asylum for medical care. We had badly underestimated the direction and cruelty of the revolutionary movement. Iran had always been a friendly nation, known for its religious tolerance. The current situation in Egypt is a similar situation in which we fear to support an ally who is losing a revolution against him.

A secret pre-dawn rescue mission of US. Marine commandos failed when their helicopter crashed into a plane in the Iranian desert. There's a movie clip on Google showing John acting as a gracious host, following Persian traditions. He warmly welcomed President Khamenei when he visited the prisoners in their compound. Speaking in Farsi, John teased the president that the Iranian tradition of welcome was so established than when he and the 51 other "guests" of the Iranian people asked to leave, the Iranian reply was "No, No, you must stay."

Forty of the 52 surviving hostages meet at West Point on each anniversary of their release. They are interested in suing Iran for compensation for their captivity but are hindered by the Algiers Accords in which the U.S. (with a gun to its head) agreed to unfreeze Iranian assets and to give immunity in exchange for the hostages' release. The issue is to be resolved in appellate courts later this year.

Note: (from **Mamie Klein** April 25. 1980) You'll be interested in knowing that Dorothy Limbert was here yesterday, visiting her mother in Hollywood.

We could not really discuss Johnny's situation in Iran because they have kept the news from her mother who is quite elderly. But you can imagine the agitation we felt with the news that broke yesterday! I spoke with Jack a few weeks ago and Becky sent me the Washington Star clipping of the interview during the Red Cross visit."

MAKING LEMONADE

When life dealt him lemons, one of the Shulkins made lemonade.

Greg Shulkin, of Montreal, suffered bacterial meningitis at age 18 in 1992. That turned into kidney failure, a stroke and a heart attack that left him dead for 12 minutes. Since then he has been partially paralyzed and legally blind.

With intensive rehabilitation therapy, he has been able to get his college degree and today supports himself traveling the world as a motivational speaker at grade schools and varied organizations.

In 2009, he was an Olympic Torch bearer and a team member of the Canadian Olympic bobsled team.

Not quite as dramatic is Jennie Shulkin's experience in tearing a shoulder ligament at age 15 while playing tennis. Surgery and physical therapy rehabilitation restored motion in the shoulder but did not relieve the pain. She continues to play tennis despite the pain as part of the rehab program. The following is a news story,

"Jennie began playing tennis at age two and a half and has thrown herself into the sport ever since. She has been the number one singles player on the Harriton tennis team since her freshman year, helping the team win the state championship in each of the last four seasons. Strong on the court and in the classroom, Jennie has a 4.94 GPA on a 4.0 scale—made possible through taking difficult honors and AP classes.

Always a competitive tennis player, Jennie won the top ranked girls tennis player in the Philadelphia area in the 10 and under division, and again in the 14 and under division as an 11 year old. She said that winning the honor again felt great, especially considering her battle with a torn labrum in her shoulder over the last two years.

Sometime during her sophomore season, Jennie sustained the shoulder injury and had to drop out of tennis competition completely to have surgery. With rehab taking longer than expected, she said she didn't know if she would ever be able to play again.

A year and a half after the surgery, she was able to return to the court. Her senior season Harriton won the state championship again as a team, and Jennie and her doubles partner Marni Blumenthal won the PIAA Class AA doubles state championship.

"It's nice to complete the cycle that I started when I was young," she said. "To come back means a lot."

Now, as the USTA's top player in the area, Jennie hopes to continue to play tennis or squash (she's ranked in the top 40 nationally) at a top-ranked college. She doesn't plan on playing professionally, but said she might want to consider going to law school instead.

Dara Welles (Aronoff) commented: "Wow! This article about Jennie came to me on a google alert. Congrats and love to you all".

I FORGIVE YOU FOR BEING CRITICAL

Sunny had a critical father and I had a critical mother so we both were experts at being critical but hated being criticized. Most of our marriage had been taken up with my being critical of her-for being critical of me–for being critical of her– etc.

Our daughter, Nedra, was a marriage counselor when she was four.

A Different Approach

Then, one day out of the clear blue, Sunny had a new game plan.

"Mark", she said, "the next time I'm critical, would you put your hand on my shoulder, look me in the eye, and say to me as sincerely as you can, 'Sunny, I forgive you for being critical?'"

I wasn't buying that! After all, I'm not stupid. Wouldn't that just give her license to be even more critical? I'm thinking,
"better she should tell me that she forgives me for being critical"–but that would seem sarcastic since most of the time I don't think I'm being critical even when I am.

But one battle weary day, I decided to experiment I put my hand on her shoulder, looked her in the eye, and stuttered as sincerely as anyone could with tongue firmly in cheek, "Sunny, I f-forg-give you for being c-critical".

And then a miracle happened. I had suddenly stopped being "critical" and had become "forgiving".

At first the "forgiving" went against my grain, but it was easier each time I sputtered Sunny's phrase. Eventually I would look forward to her criticism so that I could glory in my forgiving nature.

Aftermath

A few weeks after Sunny's giving me my mantra, our daughter Nedra surprised us with a visit just as Sunny said something critical to me. I did my *schtick* with "I forgive you for being critical". Well, Nedra almost fainted. Instead of the usual war of words, she saw my chest expand ** and in Sunny's face there was a glowing smile.

A few weeks after that, Nedra was driving with her husband, Joe, in the passenger seat and six year old Ben seat belted in the back, supposedly asleep. Nedra narrowly missed their mailbox turning into the driveway and Joe's unJoe-like expletive surprised even Joe.

Nedra said that she doesn't know where the words came from, but they flowed modulated and clear, "Joe, I forgive you for being critical".

Upon which little Ben, suddenly alert, blurted,"And Mother, I forgive you for being critical of me for the 3,050th time."

No one suspected Ben capable of such large numbers or knew that he'd even been counting. But it was obvious that he'd just heard some new words that fostered self expression.*** Ben, 20 years later, as yet he shows no sign of being critical. Hopefully the family tradition of criticizing has ended and Ben will not pass it on to his kids.

Notes:
*Constructive criticism is the practice of praising someone for an aspect of their behavior and then making suggestions about how that behavior could become even more praiseworthy. The reason it is not more effective has to do with each of us being self critical and that the forgiveness factor is required to alter that trait.

** Typical reaction of someone who has been shamed by criticism is that their chest sinks in, their chin lowers toward their chest, their cheeks flush and they go into cognitive shock. (Huh??? What are you talking about?)

THE ROCKING CHAIR

Mark and Sunny Shulkin in 1995

One day in 1995, Sunny, handed me a piece of paper. It wasn't the grocery list. It was a 10 line script that I was to memorize and perform.

Every Sunday morning at 10 am, I was to

1. Take her by the hand
2. Lead her down to the family room
3. Sit in the Boston rocker and while holding her in my arms and recite, "I will never leave you" and follow the script on and on until number 10, when I was to sing to her "YOU ARE MY SUNSHINE".

My immediate response was less than positive, "Like Hell, I'll do that". I've got radar for anyone trying to control me. I don't even control my self, more often than not. I prefer root canals to being told what to do. Bad enough that I have to obey the traffic laws let alone express love by the numbers.

It wasn't all that long after the wedding that romantic love morphed into a power struggle over "who controls who". I remember leaving the altar with the Rabbi's words reverberating, "And now two people are one"

"Yeah, and I'm the one!" I thought.

A Change of Heart

Then, in a moment of rationality, I decided to memorize her script and even add a little to it. It was the piece about holding her in my arms and saying "I'll never leave you" that got to me.

It reminded me that Sunny had been a three and a half pound "preemie" confined to an incubator for the first couple of months of her life. Back in those pre-penicillin days of the 1930's, preemies were never touched by human hands. They were bottle fed through sleeves in the side of the incubator. Infection was life threatening for infants back then.

When Sunny was able to leave the hospital, her workaholic breadwinner mother had long been back to work. Mom was warm when available but not all that available.

So, on Sunday morning, I took her by the hand and led her down to the family room. Holding her in my arms, I rocked her and told her that I loved her, that my life would be empty without her, that I was so glad that I had married her and that I would never leave her. I caressed her face and told her that her skin was smooth as silk, her teeth as white as pearls and that I loved the soft feel of her dainty hands. I would never abandon her and we would be together forever. I crooned to her,
"You are my sunshine, my only sunshine
You make me happy when skies are gray
You'll never know dear, how much I love you
Oh please, don't take my sunshine away."

Tears streamed down her cheeks. My eyes were also overflowing. I needed to hear those words as much as Sunny did. The Rabbi's pronouncement about oneness had a new meaning for me.

Children of Abandonment

Both Sunny and I were children of the abandonment that we had no way of controlling. I'd been born in 1929, shortly before Black Tuesday, the day the banks failed and the Great Depression began. To make ends meet my mother joined my father in working long hours in his one man neighborhood drug store and I seldom saw them.

Instead there was a succession of unmarried pregnant women who substituted for my mother, working for their room and board until their own baby was born. They were referred to live at our house by the church sponsored House of the Good Shepherd just before they began to "show" at four months and they left suddenly when they went into labor five months later.

I remember those who came after I was old enough to have words, words being essential for retaining thoughts and feelings.* They were warm and caring young women. I felt the loss of each of them.

Sunny and I did our Sunday ritual several more times and then Sunny said that I didn't have to do it anymore. She said that just the fact that I was willing to do it made her feel secure.

The Phone Call

I answered the phone at 11:00 pm, on a Friday night, December 26, 1995. A female voice from Saunders House, the nursing home where Sunny's mother lived, asked, "Is Mrs. Shulkin there?"

I woke Sunny with, "It's for you".

Sunny picked up the phone and looking shocked, moaned, and said "Mark! My mother's dead."

I took her by the hand and led her down to the family room. Holding her in my arms, I rocked her and told her that I loved her, that my life would be empty without her, that I was so glad that I had married her and that I would never leave her. I caressed her face and told her that her skin was smooth as silk, her teeth as white as pearls and that I loved the soft feel of her dainty hands. I would never abandon her and we would be together forever. I crooned to her, "You are my sunshine, my only sunshine",

The funeral was on a cold, dreary, rainy Sunday. It was a fitting climate for the occasion. At the graveside ceremony, the mourners were dwarfed by their big black umbrellas.

That evening, reviewing the funeral, I commented to Sunny that her sister, Zelda Kathrins, had been crying, her brother in law, Al Kathrins, had been crying, and I had been crying, but that she hadn't been crying. Sunny replied thoughtfully, "You know, Mark, you've been such a good replacement for her that I didn't need to cry".

It was nice to hear that even if it wasn't true.

LOVE AT THE AIRPORT

by Sunny Shulkin

Airports, with their comings and goings, their arrivals and departures, set the stage for love. No one doubts love at the airport.

There is something that tugs at my heart when I'm surrounded by tender farewells and grand reunions. Whenever I observe a reunion, I'm moved just being in the vicinity of the warm welcome home. And as I write this, a memory begins to surface.

I can still see myself at the age of four. I went from the safety of my home to the uncertainty of an over-night summer camp. I remember my parents dropping me off, suitcases and gear, and thinking that I'd never see them again. Then, one month later, on visiting day, I was stunned to see my mother. Here was the woman I thought I'd never see again and I galloped towards her, arms akimbo, whooping and hollering. I was beyond happy; I still had a mother.

Perhaps, I'm moved because of that memory. Or, perhaps it's the longing for a similar whoop and warm welcome from Mark. Oh, to be received with such joy!

My request to be greeted with a hug at the exit from the airplane made no sense to him. "After all," he said, "You travel on business all the time. Besides, I DO pick you up. It's just that I pick you up outside the luggage carousel. That way, I don't have to pay for parking."

His logic stopped me from complaining further. One part of me agreed with him. He *never* failed to be there at the luggage carousel. It *was* unnecessary to pay the parking fees. Maybe, what he gave me was enough. But, another part of me was so sad. I wanted what came easily for others. I wanted love at the airport.

By this time, I was getting to know myself better. I knew this: my very big wishes didn't go away. I had risked asking before. I would ask again and I would be very specific.

"Mark," I said, "I have this wish and I only need this wish granted once. My wish is that when I come home from traveling this week, you meet me at the airport gate, beam at me and hug me." Mark agreed. It seemed like a reasonable request. After all, it was just this one time.

I was away from home for several days, but finally, I was on my way back. As I stepped off the walkway from the plane into the airport, I saw Mark. He had a huge grin on his face and he called out to me warmly, "Sunny, you're home!" Then, he moved towards me and gave me a hug. It wasn't the hug I expected. I only felt one arm around me. I stepped back, shocked, and said, "Mark, where's your other arm?"

With that, he pulled his other arm from behind his back and offered me a bouquet of flowers...all too familiar flowers. "Where did you get these flowers?" I cried. Giving him no time to answer, I continued: "You pulled them from our garden, our wildflower garden. How could you!"

"Well," said Mark, defensively, "You didn't want me to spend money on flowers and parking, did you?"

We drove home in silence. The flowers were left and forgotten in the backseat where they turned straw-like, as dead as our attempt at love at the airport.

I had no idea how Mark and I could restore connection after this rupture. Several days passed. We still weren't talking and my anger settled into despair.

I had felt so alive and so hopeful that Mark was becoming more thoughtful and more responsive to me and that together we could create a truly satisfying relationship. However, I was learning by now, that my disappointment, blame and anger only guaranteed that nothing would change.

I wondered what would happen if I took ownership for my part in our latest relationship fiasco. I said to Mark,

"I let my anger over the flowers cloud the generosity you gave me in coming to the gate to welcome me home. I've done that before, rejected your love because one thing wasn't just right. I want to be able to receive love with the generosity that you show me."

"I'm glad you said that," he replied. And then he confessed. "I told the kids about your wish and they got so gung-ho, they suggested I bring you flowers and make it a really special event. I did go to a florist, but I thought even you wouldn't spend that kind of money! I never stopped to think that you didn't ask for flowers and I never stopped to think what it would mean to you to cut flowers from our garden. I need to remember *you* and your idea of a gift, not something others think you'd like."

We were learning that we didn't have to get it right or to be perfect in order to be loved. We were also beginning to trust that after a ruptured connection, repair was possible. I was learning that when one of us took ownership, it allowed the other to cross the bridge that was being extended and to re-connect. Now that kind of relationship was worth coming home to!!

Mark Weiss Shulkin MD

WHAT AUNT MARY TOLD ME

by Gailya Paliga in 1997

In 1905, Aunt Mary's father, Jacob, emigrated to America-alone. It was a grave occasion because it was felt that when someone left for America, they would never be seen again. This was the truth, too, because all the relatives who remained in Russia were killed in 1916 or 1919. (They were persecuted because of their religion.)

Since only one ticket to America could be afforded, Jacob had to work very hard when he finally reached Milwaukee to earn enough money to send for his family. He worked as a peddler/salesman selling dress-goods door to door. Even though he probably didn't eat half the time, after only nine months, he had earned enough money to buy four more boat tickets.

Meanwhile, back in Russia, Great Aunt Mary's family was left with little money and no income. They were eventually evicted from their primitive house. For their last few weeks in Russia, the family had to live in their grandfather's house. As a result, she doesn't remember what her house looked like, only her grandfather's.

Finally one day, the boat tickets came. On the day they were supposed to leave, all the aunts and uncles and cousins came to say goodbye. Everyone was sad and crying. They hugged the children and made the biggest fuss ever because Aunt Mary and her brothers were the only great grandchildren and grandchildren her relatives had, and now they were leaving.

They loaded their bundles of clothing, bedding, candlesticks, etc. onto a wagon and left Russia–never to return. Aunt Mary says she will never forget her departure as long as she lives.

There was a man driving this wagon, who was part of the underground railroad system. It was his job to sneak people across the Russian' border. The horse and wagon ride seemed endless to my great aunt. It stopped once to pick up more people, and then traveled on for another couple of days. The next step was actually crossing the border. The people were instructed that on that night they would have to travel silently, so they wouldn't be caught. Aunt Mary and her brother, Joe, each held a side of their mother's skirt. My great grandmother held the nine month old baby, Izzy, and they walked and walked—"forever"—in silence. Sometimes, she said, they had to squat down and stay very still. They finally made it through to the other side where another wagon was waiting to take them to a boat.

COLLEGE DAYS

As reported in Worcester Magazine by Jeremy Shulkin December 2010

Jeremy Shulkin

It's around 1:15 a.m. on a Sunday morning in November and a Holy Cross student I am interviewing is wearing a blazer and a pair of Sperry's boat shoes and he is sitting on the front lawn of a house on College Street.

"If you want to go to a party, there's one right there," he says, pointing to an adjacent three decker.

"But it's pretty small. Only, like, 10 or so people in there."

An unmarked police car drives by, window rolled down. The officer stares as he passes, and parks down the street. This is the fourth police car in a one-block radius.

"It's a bad weekend for parties," the student laments. "Wish I could help you out more."

In a year marked by divisive city council debates regarding divesting from Arizona and a pit bull ordinance, railing against Holy Cross has been something of a safe, unifying topic for officials.

Last week students on Caro Street created their own unique game of Spin Art by dumping a bucket of paint in the middle of the road for the tire tread of passing cars to spread. This, added to reports of public urination, hundreds of students in the streets late at night and vandalism – some witnessed by council members – has brought "conversation" about Holy Cross to a tipping point.

In the days since, a number of letters have been written between city and college officials, and made public. There are plenty of scapegoats and enough finger-pointing to go around, even if no one wants to speak publicly. A number of sources contacted for this story did not want to comment directly about Holy Cross, for fear of straining relations even further. Many did not return phone calls.

Others like to point to the student body, stereotyping the 2,900 post-teens as "spoiled richies" who care nothing about Worcester. Put them four-to-a-floor in three deckers that have been scooped up over the years by absentee landlords, and there's the combination of a house with no rules and little consequence.

On the flipside, others say the residents on the hill should have expected this when they moved to a neighborhood in a college area. After all, no one who lives there predates the school.

There's also the law-enforcement aspect. Holy Cross campus police have no jurisdiction off campus (where the problems are happening), and the Worcester Police Department, while boosting their presence on the hill over the past few weekends, have bigger issues to deal with in other parts of the city.

IMMIGRATION TO ISRAEL

by Daniel B. Shulkin

"The catastrophe which recently befell the Jewish people, the massacre of millions of Jews in Europe, was another clear demonstration of the urgency of solving the problem of its homelessness by re-establishing in Eretz-Israel the Jewish State. It would open the gates of the homeland wide to every Jew and confer upon the Jewish People the status of a fully privileged member of the community of nations."

The above is from the Declaration of Independence for the State of Israel adopted in 1948 by David Ben Gurion, the first Prime Minister of Israel.

Israel is home to the Jewish people but not many Jews of the world have always lived in Palestine. Since any Jew is welcome to return and make *aliya* to Palestine, Palestine is a society composed of immigrants from all over the world.

By coming from all over the globe, the immigrant society in Palestine is not a melting pot but rather a boiling pot. The immigrants share a common bond, but each immigrant saw a different aspect of the traditions developed in his previous country. It is these traditions boiling together that unify the country.

The plan to have Palestine be a refuge for Diaspora Jews and to allow for mass migration was originally more of a long range goal than an immediate plan. The reasons why the Jews were going to Israel was not clear cut like *Olim* (pilgrims making *aliya*) versus other immigrants. There were overlapping factors including social, cultural, religious as well as economic ones in their choosing to immigrate.

Differences of opinion arose as to whether there should be unsupervised, random mass immigration or very supervised immigration limited to people who had funds to support themselves. Baron Rothschild, a major philanthropist of the time, was opposed to mass immigration. He believed in aiding the development of Palestine with financial means and not people.

At one point, it was suggested that people send funds for an orchard and only after the orchard was productive could the people follow their funds. Then the people who would be allowed to go would be the young, healthy, capable of physical effort and preferably those who had funds to get themselves there without a family to support. They could create an ideal settlement and be leaders.

There were several different types of settlements created as models of what would come to be. Rishon Le Zion was one of the first places. It was a *moshava*- (a form of rural settlement as opposed to communal settlements like the *kibbutz*, the land and property being privately-owned).

The question became, "Was Palestine dealing with individuals or the collective fate of the Jewish people? Was it only a country for the rich who could afford to own the land or was it for Jewish settlers?" These ideas evolved from Herzl's first *aliya* that supported mass migration developing agriculture and from the second *aliya* which developed agriculture as well as the urban setting to absorb immigrants who didn't work the land. These are both still viable concepts, though most American Jews prefer to donate money rather than to immigrate.

There are also Jews who oppose the idea of Israel as a Jewish homeland. I heard one speak at NYU recently. He believes we should have awaited the coming of the Messiah.

Note: There is currently a functioning *moshava* in Wild Rose, Wisconsin where my grandfather, Mark Shulkin, as an AZA member one hot summer in the 1940's, had weeded rows of corn.

HIS LAST DECISION

by Jennifer Shulkin

Jennie Shulkin

When I heard the news, the only thought that crossed my mind was, "How could this be happening?" I was confused and shocked, but mostly, I was infuriated. I was only thirteen years old when my father unintentionally chose a grey-sky'd night to inform me that my Grand Uncle Alfred was soon to die. The reason why I was infuriated was because he did not have to die. Uncle Al was choosing to die.

Uncle Al had had a serious stroke and, as a result, could not swallow food properly. Pleading that he did not want to live in such a poor condition, he refused the feeding tube, therefore forfeiting his life. Because my father, a physician, was against this decision, and because I did not understand these situations well, I saw this as giving up. My father said Uncle Al probably only had a few weeks before he would leave us forever.

When I heard that, my life of knowing Uncle Al passed in review. While I only saw him maybe four times a year, I certainly loved him. I could not imagine family get-togethers without his aged smile and the ironic reassurance from his rough voice, deepened by a long-time cigarette addiction. At that moment, I also recall being thankful that I had given him a hug goodbye the last time I saw him, because I realized that would be the last time he would ever be able to hug me back.

Even though I was angry with Uncle Al for his choice to give up fighting for more time, I was determined to make the most of my time left with him. I urged my parents to visit him at his retirement home, and we did. One of my goals was to make him feel less alone, while another was to see if I could get him to eat or drink at all despite his immediate family's willingness to simply let him starve to death.

When I arrived at Uncle Al and Aunt Zelda's cramped apartment, Uncle Al was sitting on the couch with his shirt off and an exhausted expression comparable to how I imagine he looked at some of his lowest moments as a soldier in World War II.

Seeing my Uncle Al like this was upsetting, but for his sake, I only allowed myself to shed one or two tears. I held his hand and asked him how he was feeling. Then, knowing he was probably sick of people obsessing over his decaying health, I started talking about my life—school, tennis, family, and he started to smile. (That smile was the reason why I came.)

Uncle Al was unable to ingest anything besides applesauce and liquids and all of these were taken with a spoon. In an even weaker voice than usual, he asked to have some of his favorite drink, Diet Coke. My mother objected saying that soda was unhealthy for someone in his state, but my father argued, "Let him have what he wants." If he is going to die, at least let him die with a pleasant taste on his tongue, right? I poured a bowl of Diet Coke, filled the spoon with a fraction of the bowl's contents, and slowly inserted the spoon into Uncle Al's mouth before tipping the spoon on a gentle angle to allow the liquid to travel towards the back of his throat. I probably did this until I was told to stop.

Uncle Al's words were limited, so when he spoke, it was important. He whispered with pauses between his words, "You're going to make a great mother." I remember this as one of the highest compliments I have ever received. The rest of the room was silent and wide-eyed as they watched my apparent (but artificial) ease in such a depressing situation.

During the period in which Uncle Al was dying, I learned several valuable lessons. The first was that it is important to appreciate what we have. I stopped focusing so much on my geometry grade and how nasty thirteen-year-old girls could be. Another lesson is the significance of family. Family is comfort and support in dire situations, and sometimes, it can even bring joy to the person in need. Evoking a smile from a man who was at one of the most miserable moments in his life meant the world to me. From that day out, I looked to bring smiles to people's faces, especially people that could use those few moments of happiness the most.

Probably the most vital message I discovered from my experiences with Uncle Al was that I could be there for and do something for someone in extremis (even if only spoon feeding Diet Coke). While I certainly was not fearless, I had experienced some courage and felt a certain strength.

People say, "What doesn't kill you makes you stronger." Well, sometimes it does kill you, but it makes those around you stronger.

ERASER TATTOOS

by Jennifer Shulkin and Merle Bari MD

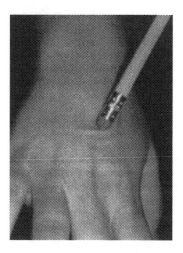

A 13-year-old boy from inner city Philadelphia presented with an infected "tattoo" on his right forearm. On examination, he had multiple hypo-pigmented scars on his extremities. When asked about the scars, the patient appeared embarrassed and stated that they were tattoos, which he created with an eraser from a pencil. To make a tattoo, he rubbed the eraser across the skin while applying strong pressure for an extended time. The friction would eventually abrade the skin until it became red and bled. The wound would scab, leaving a permanent hypo-pigmented scar.

Seeing teenagers with tattoos is not unusual in a dermatology practice. Up to 30% of Americans under age 30 have tattoos. In Canada, 8% of high school students have at least 1 tattoo.[1] The types of tattoos available range from temporary to permanent (e.g. professionally inked). Homemade eraser tattoos—hypo-pigmented scars in various shapes or letters on the arms and legs—appear to be a phenomenon among elementary and middle school students in the United States. These tattoos are easily accessible, require no parental consent, and have no cost barrier. The motivation for teenagers to apply these tattoos may be artistic expression, peer pressure, or the need to be accepted. Some teens report that their tattoos were applied against their will by another student.

Tattoos can signal a troubled teen. Adolescents who use painful methods to permanently scar themselves may be at risk for other adverse behaviors, such as eating disorders, drug use, and violence.[5] The type of tattoo and the design can also be meaningful. The design of the tattoo may reveal a gang name or slogan. Gang-related tattoos often symbolize membership or the gang's beliefs; however, they may represent an act of violence. For instance, a tattoo in the shape of a teardrop may indicate murder.

Most cases of homemade tattoos tend to be a form of self-expression for peer acceptance rather than a form of self-mutilation. Teens with homemade tattoos warrant a social and/or psychological assessment to rule out abuse or a psychological disorder. If after this assessment, a teen is suspected of risky behavior, he or she can be counseled or referred to social services. If the tattoo is merely a form of self-expression, the clinician can discuss other ways patients can express themselves that do not pose a medical risk of inflammation, infection, or scarring.

LIKE NIGHT AND DAY

by David Shulkin MD
New England Journal of Medicine- May 2008

David Shulkin

Lately, I've been coming to work at midnight. You see, I've begun making late-night administrative rounds at the hospital where I am president and chief executive officer. No, I'm not nostalgic for my harrowing days as a resident. Rather, these middle-of-the-nighters are part of an initiative of mine intended to address a matter that is of increasing concern at hospitals throughout the country: the stark discrepancy in quality between daytime and nighttime inpatient services.

Like many hospital executives, I've come to appreciate the fact that I work in two distinct places, though they share the same address. One is a hospital that operates from approximately 7 a.m. until 7 p.m., Monday through Friday. The other is a hospital that operates in the evening, through the night, and on weekends. Although these facilities appear to be one and the same, they in fact represent two very different medical environments.

The weekday hospital has a full administrative team, department chairs and service chiefs, experienced nurse managers, and a full complement of professional staff. The off-hours hospital, on the other hand, rarely, if ever, has senior managers present. Nurse-to-patient ratios are significantly lower. Even the number of residents is considerably lower — certainly lower than during my days of training because of mandated work-hour restrictions.

The positive spin on these differences is that we are trying to achieve a calmer and quieter environment at night and on the weekend so that our patients can rest and recuperate. But there are serious downsides. Silent hospital corridors can also reflect sparse staffing and a lack of institutional leadership, which make important hospital services and consultative expertise difficult to obtain. This discrepancy in provider care between daytime and nighttime inpatient services is a matter of growing concern to health care professionals, because people get sick 24 hours a day. In fact, 50 to 70% of patients are admitted to the hospital at night or on the weekend.

The consequences of service deficiencies during off-hours include higher mor*tality* and readmission rates more surgical complications, and more medical errors. Given the health care industry's renewed focus on ensuring patient safety and providing high-quality medical care, why hasn't the situation changed at the "other hospital"?

Instituting longer hours for care providers is not a reasonable solution to the problem, since medical professionals who work for too long at a stretch become fatigued and make more errors. Another major obstacle is the nursing shortage. More-experienced nurses understandably choose desirable day shifts. As a result, night and weekend shifts are filled with a greater percentage of temporary or agency nursing staff, many of whom have less training and less familiarity with the hospital.

This brings me back to my midnight rounds. They are proving to be a good way to help me understand and address the concerns of our off-hours staff. Recently, I surveyed our evening and weekend hospital managers and was surprised to learn that many of them had never before been asked their opinions. Improvement takes time. The wheels are turning slowly, but lately, I'm more confident that we are moving in the right direction even if it costs me a little sleep.

HEART AND SOUL OF JEWISH MARRIAGE

by Nedra Fetterman Ph.D.

Nedra and Joseph Fetterman

I propose a workshop that integrates Jewish metaphor and tradition into the fabric of a marriage workshop since Judaism contains a rich body of teachings about marriage. A sense of wholeness, healing and the meaning of a couple's life together is a very Jewish idea. At the heart of this workshop would be the idea that healing can begin when things seem most broken and shattered.

The ideas in this proposal are the product of my longtime experience with *"The Getting the Love You Want Workshop"* as a workshop leader and a faculty member of Imago Relationship Therapy International. My own deep spiritual longings were met by the profound nature of Imago Relationship Therapy and they compelled me to embark on a spiritual journey that is still unfolding. The training I received as a psychologist, psycho-therapist and on the frontlines as a partner in a 30 year marriage is also the foundation for this proposal.

Imago Therapy provides a structure and a set of tools that keeps intimate partnerships alive and blooming. The challenges inherent in marriage can launch a couple on a healing journey that leads to a more conscious, loving and satisfying life. My marriage presented me with these challenges as well as the warmth, acceptance and sense of humor that has made my journey life-altering and rewarding.

Day One: Safety

Unfortunately, intimacy is a trauma trigger. The closer we get to a loved one, the more likely unfinished business or unmet needs from the past emerge into the present-day relationship. The purpose for this emerging is the unconscious longing for needs to be understood and/or met and injuries to be repaired.

In Jewish mysticism, the sacred work of healing and repair occurs through *tikkun olam and tikkun ha'nefesh:* healing the world and our individual souls. "Since each individual person is a microcosm of the world, every act of *tikkun ha'nefesh* is of great, if not cosmic, importance."

Kabalistic myth uses the image of shattered vessels as a healing metaphor. We are both broken and whole. The myth of the broken tablets of Sinai also underscores the importance of broken and whole since according to legend the Israelites carried both the broken set and the whole set into the ark for the rest of their journey through the desert.

Defensive marital routines, which include distancing and pursuing, lead to the worn-out steps of the dance of intimacy. In Jewish mysticism, it is thought that spiritual awakening begins with learning how to navigate through the dark. In Israel, the new day begins in the evening, in the dark. The biblical account of creation stresses that "there was evening and then there was morning." Before there could be light, darkness had to be created. Couples, therefore, need to learn to navigate through darkness, danger and defensive routines and to transform those defensive postures into ones that create light and safety.

Day Two: Aliveness and Pleasure

For a relationship to become truly safe, blame and projection must end and partners must become a source of pleasure to one another as well as a source of safety. The Hebrew word for oneness – *echad* – comes from the same root as the word for joy – *chedva*. What is being suggested here is that more joy is possible when we are aware of our oneness and deep connection.

A key idea here is that relationships have the capacity to move us towards our greater wholeness and internal unity as well as to feeling at one with the other.

Growth occurs in a relationship through stretching into lost or missing pieces of the self. We often partner with someone who carries our missing pieces. We are therefore attracted to them since the search for wholeness is uncompromising and non-negotiable. Some key ideas are:

1. Contained within attraction are the seeds of the power struggle since our lost self was only lost because it was forbidden, dangerous or unacceptable. So we gave up a part of ourselves to maintain our connection to mom/dad and the family. We then fall in love with that lost part that is in the partner and eventually we oppose that part by trying to extinguish it in our partner since that was what was done to us.

2. Partners will be frustrated with one another in the area of their missing selves and criticize one another for not being emotional enough, smart enough, assertive enough, sexual enough, etc. Each of these frustrations or criticisms point to a lost or wounded part of ourselves.

3. The story of Exodus is a leaving of the constriction of Egypt and traveling to the Promised Land, a place of fuller consciousness. The desert is the power struggle and the Promised Land is mature love.

4. The Hebrew word for Egypt is *Mitzrayim,* meaning narrow straits or a tight place. Jewish mystics see *Mitzrayim* not only as a geographical place but as a symbol of constricted consciousness. This is similar to the Imago concept of reclaiming the lost self and returning energy to the more authentic core of the self. This process may be thought of as t*eshuvah,* returning to a truer nature.

It is that truer nature, a return to our sense of original wholeness, aliveness and oneness that allows the flow of loving energy between partners to flourish.

SAVING THE GULF COAST

by Benjamin Fetterman
(while spending a month in Alabama during September 2010.)

Ben Fetterman

As many of us struggle with a stagnant economy, many residents on the Gulf Coast are dealing with a bigger issue, a dying economy. Although BP's Deepwater Horizon oil rig was capped over two months ago, and the relief well has been fully completed, the effects of the spill are still hitting the coast. These economic effects are not measured in gallons of oil or dispersants; they are not measured in dead wildlife or fish kills, but rather in percentages of lost business. In the small beach town of Gulf Shores, Alabama, the economy is slowly deteriorating. Businesses of all sizes are on life support because of the lost tourism caused by BP's spill. The spill ravaged tourism industry has a trickle down affect.

Since the beaches were closed this summer, house rentals and hotel room reservations were cancelled at alarming rates. Rental companies still cannot fill their houses because of the lingering psychological impact the spill has left on potential and past renters. Since the Gulf Shores economy relies so heavily on its tourism industry, many businesses along the coastline were crushed economically.

Many people in Gulf Shores, Alabama have lost almost everything. Most businesses are down 70-80% of their usual traffic. Because Gulf Shores' economy is 90% tourism, businesses rely on the summer season to get them through the entire year. Some stores have gone out of business and locals believe many more will close their doors over the winter.

This is why the BP claims are so important. People need these claims to sustain their livelihood. But here in lies the problem. Many who receive BP claims will be forfeiting the right to participate in a future lawsuit. Also, others may be denied a claim for various reasons: lack of past income records, improper tax filings, far proximity from the beach amongst many other reasons.

Denial of claims could cause a lot of anger. Locals are concerned that the denial of a claim could lead to more suicides in this area. It is a very sensitive issue. I can only pray that BP does right by the people of the Gulf Coast and provides them the income lost by this spill.

Family Correspondence

Gloria Fish wrote: Jan 1979
"Your nephew Jim Shulkin is a friend of my daughter's at the University of Wisconsin. Diana recognized the name Shulkin as my grandmother's maiden name. Since we are both genealogy buffs, perhaps we could fill in some missing links? My great grandparents were Gertrude {Shafton) and Chaim (Charles Hyman) Shulkin. Are we related?"

Reply: Your great great grandfather Joshua Sockne and my great great grandfather Isaac Shulkin were brothers.

Max Levine wrote March 3, 1979 (excerpted) "I was shocked beyond words when I heard that you were planning to write the "roots" about the Schulkin family. I did not know you were planning to write a novel and smearing your branch of Grandpa Malech's family.

Grandpa was not as bad as you pictured him to be. He sent your father thru college, he also helped him buy his first drug store. So he was not the miser that you depict him to be.

Leah Lubchick wrote: (translated Nov 1979)
"Shulkina and now Lubchik, Leah Girshevna, that's me. We were living in Polotsk, Vitebsk guberniya and then we moved to Mogilev where we are living now.

My husband Avram, and daughter Elka died during the war. She left a daughter. I had a brother named Zoosha. He died a long time ago, but left a daughter, Polya. My eldest brother Itzhak, died in 1972 but he left a daughter, Rosa, and a son Abraham. And that is all that is left of the Shulkin family. I was the youngest. My birthday is May 25, 1900. I will soon be 80 years old."

Mamie Klein wrote April 28, 1980: "I remember your grandparents well. We visited them in Milwaukee when I was a child and I remember the house quite well. In fact Malech attended my wedding in 1940. I visited your parents in Madison a couple of times. My very best to your mother.

I was interested to learn that the Shulkins consider themselves Litvaks –but not in my family. My parents always insisted they were White Russians and it's a running discussion I've had with Joe all our married life. He calls me a Litvak."

Warren Cohen wrote May 14, 1993 "My mother Dora still lives in Massena, even though she has a winter home near Ft. Lauderdale. I had never heard of the blood libel story in Massena though I was the best of friends with my grandfather Jake Shulkin. As a child I used to go on fishing trips with him on the St Lawrence River. He told me about sweatshops in New York and pogroms in Russia but he never mentioned the 1928 blood libel. Growing up in Massena I never experienced anti Jewish prejudice.

One day about 10 years ago I happened upon the <u>Incident at Massena</u> in a Judaic bookstore. You can imagine how amazed I was to read about people who I had known as a child. Jake had conferred with J.J. Kaufman and Joe Stone during the crisis."

Kaufman had opened a clothing store in Massena in 1898. I remember as a small child seeing him in the *Schul.* Joe Stone died before I was born but I remember seeing his memorial plaque in the Synagogue. I remember his widow and her brother Eli Friedman who was a very old man when the book was published. My mother says he'd still be living if he hadn't been run over by a car."

Rose Siegel wrote March 1. 1998: "I am the daughter of Edith Silverman, granddaughter of Rose Rosen Zimmermann. I have been trying to put together the Zimmermann family tree for about a year. Recently I wrote to Minnie Surkin, the oldest cousin of our generation. Friday I received a letter from her with Xeroxed copies from your book "Search for the Family".

A bit about the Zimmermann clan; Mom and Dad are still going strong, They are about 15 years retired and have done a good bit of traveling. Dad still drives and they are out of the house most days. "

Jackie Shulkin wrote May 6, 2000 "I find this so exciting. My husband is

Mike Shulkin. His father William Shulkin passed away two years ago. He came from Sioux City and moved to Spokane and then Seattle where Mike was born.

Abraham Shulkin came to America and then sent for his wife, The story goes that she placed he children as packages on the back of a wagon to get across the border. One of the children fell out and she had to go back to Russia to find the package. She found him in a ditch on the side of the road. That would be Mike the youngest of Abraham's children. (Grandpa Mike to us), Mike was married to Sophia Swanson, of the Swanson Food family and they were very well off.

There is a group of Shulkins in the Boston area but they are sure they are not related to us."

Donna Kooler wrote: Dec 2004
I am from the Sioux City branch. My grandmother was Fannie Sherman married to Ben Sherman. My mother Rose married Joseph Harris, I have two sisters, Lucille Tee and Sandra Koch. I've been married to Douglas Kooler for over 50 years and we have two children, Jim Kooler and Basha Hanner. If I can be of further help, let me know.

Ronna Schulkin wrote in 2009, "Thanks so much for all you've done for us Schulkins! My grandfather, Morris (Maurice), married Rena Meyers, born in Omaha. He had two brothers, Solomon and Samuel who was a physician. He had a sister Fannie and I think one named Rosa and some other sisters.

The original spelling of Schulkin was Shulkin. I think my grandfather might be the only one who changed to the Sch, not sure why. My grandfather and all his siblings except for Samuel were born in Kopyl near Minsk. Sam was born in Wisconsin. So the family must have originally lived in Wisconsin, had Sam, then moved to Sioux City.

Trudy Okmin was Miss Iowa as a Shulkin in 1960.She is my father's first cousin but I have never met her."

Reply: Malech Schulkin added the c to the Sh in German speaking Milwaukee so the name seemed more like Schultz which was a common name in Milwaukee. Other Shulkins spelled it Sj or just S as in Sulkin. My father took the c out during the Second World War because he didn't want to seem German.

Peggy and Ron Shulkin

Ron Shulkin wrote in 2009: "My father's father, Ruben Shulkin, antecedent of the Chicago Shulkins who came from Szarkowszczyzna in Belarus, was a tailor. His brothers all seemed to be tailors also. Their sons ended up owning dry cleaners for the most part."

Tamara Levinson wrote in Dec 2009. "Hi, I am Tamara Levinson Schulkin from Montevideo, Uruguay. Our branch came from the Ucraine to Argentina in the early 20th century. My mother, aunt and uncles were born in Tucuman, Argentina. My grandparents moved to Paysandu, Uruguay around 1930. The family name Rosen rings a bell."

Veronica Schulkin wrote in Jan 2010, "Hola! como andas los Schulkin?? Everything all right? I am Vero from Argentina! Nice to meet you!"

Marcia Sky wrote in Feb 2010
"Am I related to any of the Shulkins in the Chicago area? I recently moved to Chicago from Denver where my brother Gary Sky still lives. My cousin, Shellie Shulkin, (from Seattle) posted an extensive history of our family tree. Shellie's father, Jerry Shulkin ("Sonny"), and my mother, Doris Sky, editor of the Intermountain Jewish news, one of the nation's largest religious newspapers for decades, were brother and sister and grew up in Minot, North

Dakota. We had family who settled in Sioux City, Iowa, in Montana and California."

Reply: My great great grandfather Isaac, Gloria Fish' s and your great great grandfather Joshua Sockne and Ron Shulkin of Chicago's great great grandfather. Lepke, were brothers.

Marc Shulkin

Marc Shulkin wrote in 2010, "Hey Shulkins, I'm writing to you from Melbourne Australia. If you're wondering, I don't have a pet Kangaroo or anything like that, hee- hee. I'm 20 yrs old and Jewish.

I'm studying a double business degree at Monash University and work for two promotion companies. My Father is from New York and his parents are Holocaust survivors from Russia and Poland, if you have anything in common with the information above, add me and let me know."

Helene Shulkin commented in 2010. "I married into the Shulkin tribe, but my children are genetic Shulkins. I think they would like to connect to the family. (I have been a Shulkin since 1961, does that count for something?)"

Helene Shulkin

Sam Gahr wrote: "Our family were friends of the Shulkins who were peddlers and went to the Russian temple on 12th and Garfield. They'd always call me"Gajer" by our original name.

You have heard of the story that I used to climb piled up tires and pick up some moonshine from your zadeh Shulkin on about 7th and Galena. The tires were stacked in his back yard. We lived on 11th and Galena."

Family Photo Gallery

(Relationships of people in the photos are available on www.shulkinfamily.myheritage.com)

Martin Kathrins ansd Adi Kathrins 2010

Adam Goldberg and Dana Kathrins 2010

Michael Sattell and Leanna Shulkin 2010

David and, Merle Shulkin 2009

Joe, Nedra, Ben Fetterman and Jennifer Kurzman 2010

Bob, Elise, and Gailya Paliga 2008

Donald Shulkin and Lilian Shulkin 2000

Daniel Shulkin and Lexi Bari and her friend Danny 2010

Jerome, Max and Doris Sky 1933

Doris and Arnold Sky circ 1978

Randall Shulkin, Sandra shulkin, and Pamella Ellis

The next ten pages are left blank for placement of family pictures.

References

Boszenmenyi-Nagz, I & Spark, G, <u>Invisible Loyalties</u>, Brunner/Mazel, 1984

Conner, Susan, <u>I Remember When</u>, Jewish Federation of Sioux City, 1985

Friedman, Saul, <u>Incident at Massena</u>, Stein and Day, 1937

Gittleman, Sol, <u>From Shetl to Suburbia</u>, Beacon Press, 1978

Porello, R, <u>The Rise and Fall of the Cleveland Mafia</u>, Barricade Books,1995

Rosenbam. Lisa, <u>A Day of Small Beginnings</u>, Little/Brown, 2006

Sack, S. and Shulkin, M, <u>Search for the Family</u>, Marsal.Press, 1980
    (610) 667-7645

Sadowsky, Sandy, <u>My Life in the Jewish Mafia,</u> Putnam , 1992

Sand, Shlomo, <u>The Invention of the Jewish People</u> Verso, 2009

Shulkin, Mark W, <u>The Golden Washboards,</u> Iuniverse 2007
    (800) 288-4677

Tokayer, M. and Swartz, M., <u>Desperate Voyagers-The Fugu Plan,</u> Dell Publishing, 1979

Post Script

My boyhood friend Sam Gahr, who later married my cousin Rona Borkon, reminded me that my mother's family the Weisses were not Litvaks as the Shulkins were.

The Weisses claimed they were not Gallitzianers but White Russians (*Rushishes*). They spoke a slightly different dialect of Yiddish than the Litvaks did, pronouncing the vowels a little differently. Like they said *"pitter"* instead of *"putter"* for butter. and "keegle" for "kugel".

Sam Gahr says, "My impression of Gallitzianers was that if you shook hands with them, then you should count your fingers. I always thought people had a bad impression of them." The relationship between Litvaks and Gallitzianers was reminiscent of the Hatfields and the McCoys.

Litvaks were Mishnagim who opposed the more emotional and mystical Hassidim, like Saul and Harry Edelman in the Fugu Affair and the ultra orthodox Haredim like Rabbi Dovid Weiss pictured in Daniel Shulkin's article on Immigration to Israel. They were a more intellectual, Torah studying variation of the religion and they were known to be more authoritarian and dogmatic than the others.

In the synagogue Litvaks prayed standing rock still only their lips moving and they sat down during the Friday night Kiddush service. The others rocked while praying, the joyous sounds of happy holidays overflowing the temple walls.

Litvaks were thought to be "cold fish" by the Gallitzianers which brings up what Wikipedia describes as the "gefilte fish line" Litvak food is more plain and savory than the rich, heavily sweetened, spicier Gallitzianer food. Pehaps that's related to a genetic hypercholesterolemia in Litvaks.

At any rate, as I child and even today I prefer the meaty sweet and sour spiced cabbage borscht to the cold bland spinach borscht my father liked. My mother made a red pepper coated oniony and sugar sweetened gefilte fish beyond comparison with the tasteless white chunks Manischewitz puts in jars on supermarket shelves these days.

The rigid devotion to Torah explains Grandpa Malech's concern in the Circumcision story as well as more flexible Hasssidic Rabbi Twersky's willingness to compromise in resolving the conflict.

Not all Shulkins are Jewish. I've been in communication with Christian Schulkins families on the Isle of Wight, in London, in the Pennsylvania Dutch Country, and a Baptist Schulkins family in Montreal. The recent newspaper publicity about the legal issues involving the demolition of the old Shulkin and Slavin Furniture Store in Massena New York reminded me that in doing phone book searches for Shulkins in the 1970's, a Catholic priest named Shulkin surfaced. A phone call to him was rewarded with the story of his coming to Massena as an immigrant and seeing Shulkin on the furniture store sign he exchanged his long Polish name for a more "standard" American one.

About the Author

Mark W. Shulkin MD is a founding member of the Philadelphia Jewish Genealogical Society. He presented "Why Do Jewish Genealogy?" at the first meeting of the International Jewish Genealogy Society in Jerusalem, Israel.

Co-author of SEARCH FOR THE FAMILY, Marsal Press, 1980 and author/editor of THE GOLDEN WASHBOARDS, iUniverse Press, Dr. Shulkin is a Distinguished Life Fellow of the American Psychiatric Association, a Diplomat of the American Board of Psychiatry and Neurology, Inc., Emeritus Clinical Assistant Professor of Psychiatry at the Drexel University College of Medicine, Emeritus Clinical Instructor and Workshop Presenter for Imago Relationship Therapy International, Inc., Past President of the Delaware County Medical Society and for many years Editor of the Bulletin of the Delaware County Medical Society.

Index